QUICK EMOTIONAL INTELLIGENCE ACTIVITIES FOR BUSY MANAGERS

Quick EMOTIONAL INTELLIGENCE ACTIVITIES FOR BUSY MANAGERS

50 Team Exercises That Get Results in Just 15 Minutes

ADELE B. LYNN

AMACOM

American Management Association

New York | Atlanta | Brussels | Chicago | Mexico City | San Francisco

Shanghai | Tokyo | Toronto | Washington, D. C.

Special discounts on bulk quantities of AMACOM books are available to corporations, professional associations, and other organizations. For details, contact Special Sales Department, AMACOM, a division of American Management Association, 1601 Broadway, New York, NY 10019.
Tel.: 800-250-5308. Fax: 518-891-2372.
E-mail: specials@amanet.org
Website: www.amacombooks.org/go/specialsales
To view all AMACOM titles go to www.amacombooks.org

Library of Congress Cataloging-in-Publication Data

Lynn, Adele B.
Quick emotional intelligence activities for busy managers / Adele Lynn.
p. cm.
Includes bibliographical references and index.
ISBN-10: 0-8144-0895-8
ISBN-13: 978-0-8144-0895-7
1. Teams in the workplace—Problems, exercises, etc. 2. Emotional intelligence—Problems, exercises, etc. I. Title.

HD66.L96 2007
658.4′022019—dc22 2006020591

Printed in the United States of America.

Printing number

10 9

Contents

Acknowledgments

I express heartfelt thanks to the community of colleagues, friends, and family who wrote this book.

Jacquie Flynn, my editor at AMACOM, thanks for a great idea.

Bill, we keep doing this. Thank you for your support and for loving me in my least emotionally intelligent moments. Janele, my muse, thank you for your constant source of inspiration.

I offer special thanks to my Dream Team—Char Kinder and Emily Schultheiss—who nurture and challenge me to live my dreams. This book is evidence that the Dream Team lives its mission.

Andrea Sheperd, thanks for your help with this manuscript. It's been a pleasure.

I am so grateful to many colleagues whose brains must be sore from my constant picking at them, and who generously gave their time and expertise to test these concepts with their clients.

My clients have allowed me to fully practice the ideas in this book. Their faith in me and my work and their permission to enter their places of business allowed me to constantly refine and develop the concepts contained on these pages.

I express my gratitude to my parents and to my brother and friend, Karl, who are also intimately familiar with my shortcomings in the area of emotional intelligence but somehow love me anyway. Thanks to my new friend Babe. And lastly, thanks to God for calling me to my purpose and for standing beside me each day as I attempt to live it.

And finally, goodbye to Abby, and to my friend and mentor, Hal Swart.

Introduction

No matter how outstanding or knowledgeable an individual performer may be, if he or she doesn't have the skills to function as a team player, the goals of the unit will probably suffer. Teamwork skills are rooted in the team members' emotional intelligence. It's how people interact that determines how effectively they work together. What people say and do, how they say it, what they fail to say or do, and how they engage or avoid conflict, all contribute to team interactions. These interaction skills require highly self-aware individuals who understand their impact on the team. The most common question I am asked is, "How do you improve someone's self-awareness?" The answer to this question, which is the fundamental key to improved teamwork, is by improving emotional intelligence. The doorway to greater emotional intelligence is self-awareness. You can't be a team player until you have passed the threshold of this doorway. Therefore, it is the intention of this book to help build emotional intelligence and raise the self-awareness level of your team so that your team members understand their impact on one another and behave in a way that constitutes successful interactions.

Why? Why should you care about whether or not your team members are self-aware and understand their impact on one another? Who cares whether people get along? I'm sure you have heard and may even subscribe to the philosophy, "We're not here to like one another; we're here to get the job done." So true. And we're not proposing these activities so that people like one another. But the literature is filled with examples and research that support the fact that people's interaction skills translate to getting the job done. As a leader, you can no longer ignore the fact that people's teamwork skills are an important part of the job.

Many individuals in organizations, however, don't realize that a whole set of skills related to teamwork is required in addition to their technical or job skills. Every manager, supervisor, or project leader can tell you that when people are working together to get the job done, rather than acting from their individual interests and needs, the workday goes smoother, and productivity and quality are enhanced. But these interaction skills that lead to good teamwork aren't included in the textbooks and the training manuals. Our training efforts focus on how to do a job, not how to do a job while working as part of a team. This book will give managers, supervisors, and team leaders, quick tools for helping team members improve their emotional intelligence, so the team can successfully accomplish its goals by interacting in a way that promotes productivity rather than detracts from it. Although this book may not cure long-term ills of seriously damaged teams, it can go a long way to helping team members understand what it takes to succeed.

The exercises in this book are based on *The EQ Difference: A Powerful Plan for Putting EQ to Work* by Adele B. Lynn. *The EQ Difference* outlines a seven-step process for improving one's emotional intelligence. The activities in this book will help team members by giving them practical ways to look at their own behavior within the context of the team. Some of the activities are designed to help team members gain self-understanding and insight into their behaviors and how those behaviors affect their team members, while other activities are designed to give team members new skills. Still others are designed to strengthen and develop relationships among team members and increase their appreciation of one another. Although the focus is to improve emotional intelligence within the context of the team, most individuals will find this information useful and transferable to their personal lives as well. Becoming more self-aware and understanding our impact on others can improve our relationships with family and friends, as well as our relationships at work. Because of this, most people will see the benefit of this information beyond the scope of work. As the leader/facilitator, being able to draw on this benefit will make your job easier.

Each activity relates to one of the steps to improving emotional intelligence outlined in *The EQ Difference.* The seven steps to improved emotional intelligence are:

1. Observe—Observation requires us to gain a complete understanding of how we think, feel, and behave, and how we impact others. By

understanding ourselves and our impact on others, we are better able to determine how we interact with our team members, and we can determine if those interactions could be improved. Many times, team members are unaware of how others perceive their actions. This is an important step to improve self-awareness. This book is filled with activities that will help people become more self-aware.

2. Interpret—Interpretation requires us to identify our common patterns of thinking, feeling, and behaving within our team environments. Over time, as people work together, interaction patterns are formed. These patterns, once established, are difficult to break. They are impossible to break if people don't understand the patterns. This step helps people understand their common patterns in interacting with others. Several activities in this book are designed to help the team think about and understand the common patterns of behavior and how those patterns may be helpful or hurtful to the team. This step adds a deeper level of self-awareness because it sets the process in motion for breaking patterns and establishing new goals related to our behavior.

3. Pause—This step is a period of thoughtful pause that allows us to consider how to interact with others for the good of the team. Thinking before speaking is something that everyone should practice. For some people, this simple step of pause is the difference between positive interactions with others and negative interactions. This book contains several activities that will help people be aware and practice this skill. Sometimes, this step alone, causes a dramatic shift in behavior. When people are able to stop and think, they often regulate their own behavior.

4. Direct—This step allows us to form a thoughtful action, rather than a reaction, to an event or circumstance within the team. This step is about thoughtfully determining what action to take rather than reacting to a particular situation or person. Sometimes people just don't know what alternative behaviors they could practice that would improve team interactions. Several activities will help people determine how to redirect their behavior to improve team interaction. Team members learn new ways of behaving that will help improve their interactions.

5. Reflect—Reflection requires us to think about our interactions and form valuable learning that we can use in future interactions.

Learning how to reflect can dramatically change our behavior. Several activities in this book require people to practice reflection and apply it to improve team interactions. People will be asked to reflect on their own behavior, as well as the group's behavior. As the team practices reflection, self-awareness improves dramatically.

6. Celebrate—Celebration requires us to affirm positive interactions and reinforce the likelihood of future positive interactions. Teams that celebrate the positive interactions and positive attributes of team members are more likely to interact positively in the future. Activities that affirm and celebrate the team and team members are included in this book.

7. Repeat—Each interaction allows us to repeat our lessons learned. The advantage of working together is that each day brings new opportunities to practice and improve our working relationships.

All of the activities support one or more of the seven steps. In this book, we have prepared "A Guide to the 50 Activities" in Chapter 1. The steps are identified for easy reference so the leader/facilitator knows which activity relates to which step.

CHAPTER 1

A GUIDE TO THE 50 ACTIVITIES

Table 1-1 is designed to help you determine the appropriate activity for your next team meeting. For each activity, the table indicates the appropriate step(s) in the 7-Step Guide, the Level of Risk, the Purpose, and a Quick Synopsis, so you can decide at a glance which activity best suits your objective. We advise that you begin with some low-risk activities that will help your team become familiar with the concepts of emotional intelligence. For more information about selecting activities, see Chapter 3.

TABLE 1-1 50 Activities: A Quick Overview

Activity	Page Number	7-Step Guide	Level of Risk	Purpose	Quick Synopsis
EQ 1 Mood Check	27	1	Low	To improve understanding of mood	Put stickers on mood/emotion chart. Discuss impact on team
EQ 2 I Can Top That	31	2	Medium	Explore negative nature of competition	"That's nothing; let me tell you about . . ." Topics selected by facilitator

(continued)

TABLE 1-1. *(continued)*

Activity	Page Number	7-Step Guide	Level of Risk	Purpose	Quick Synopsis
EQ 3 Lead Balloons	34	2-3	High	Identify unresolved conflict	Identify and discuss sources of team conflict
EQ 4 When Things Go Wrong	37	2	Medium	Identify team M.O.s	Discuss team's M.O.s related to several different scenarios, such as defeated, under pressure, overworked
EQ 5 Helium Balloons	40	1	Medium	Develop awareness of positive interactions among team members	Take turns with each team member—state something he/she does that is uplifting to team
EQ 6 Hair Triggers or Hot Buttons	43	1	High	Identify triggers and impact	Unfinished sentences given to group by facilitator to help people understand their triggers and inform other team members
EQ 7 Spirit Killers	46	1	Low–Medium	Increase awareness of potential spirit killers	Brainstorm a list of possible spirit killers
EQ 8 UP	49	1	Low	Energize the group	Physical movements —repeat and celebrate when the group succeeds
EQ 9 Strung Tight	51	2	High	Identify personal M.O.s related to stress	Reflective exercise—think about occasions that cause stress and how you behave under stress
EQ 10 Team Trophies	54	5-6	Low	Identify accomplishments of the team and celebrate	Brainstorm accomplishments—both results and team interactions

Activity	Page Number	7-Step Guide	Level of Risk	Purpose	Quick Synopsis
EQ 11 Thank You for the Gifts	57	5-6	Medium	Recognize skills of team members	Use gift cards and gift bags to help team members recognize each other's skills
EQ 12 Who Said That?	61	2	Medium	Recognize "Voices"	Use worksheet to identify voices that lead to positive and negative behaviors
EQ 13 Choir Director	66	4	Medium	Help people recognize power to choose thoughts/voices	Have group members play roles related to positive and negative voices
EQ 14 Five Team Strengths	70	2-5	Low	Obtain 360 feedback on team strengths	Ask outsiders to identify Five team strengths. Team members also give strengths/compare
EQ 15 Five Team Weaknesses	74	2-5	High	Obtain 360 feedback on team weaknesses	Ask outsiders to identify Five team weaknesses. Team members also give weaknesses/compare
EQ 16 Speak Up	78	1-4	Medium	Give all members equal speaking time	Use a talking stick to indicate who has the floor. Explore reasons why some people don't speak up
EQ 17 Keep Your Eye on the Eye	81	1	High	Become aware of eye contact and impact of eye contact on others	Video tape members to determine how they use eye contact and the impact
EQ 18 My Dirty Dozen	84	4	High	Identify and share "Dirty Dozen"	Review "Dirty Dozen" and share most common ones with teammates
EQ 19 Search Warrants for the Dirty Dozen	88	4	High	Observe "Dirty Dozen" in teammates and give feedback	Use mock search warrants to give to teammates when caught thinking "Dirty Dozen"

(continued)

TABLE 1-1. *(continued)*

Activity	Page Number	7-Step Guide	of Risk	Purpose	Level Quick Synopsis
EQ 20 PFAT Self-Scan	92	1-2	High	Give group members a 4-point check sheet to use as a self-scan during conflict	Give group a controversial topic to debate so team members can perform self-scan
EQ 21 PFAT Group Scan	97	1-2	High	Give group members a 4-point check sheet to use as a group scan during conflict	Give group a controversial topic to debate so team can perform group scan
EQ 22 People and Perceptions	102	4	Low	Identify preconceived ideas about people	Show pictures or headlines and ask people to jot down their initial reactions or first impressions
EQ 23 Tuning In	105	1-2	Low	Increase awareness of internal dialogue and its impact on behavior	Give team worksheet and stop discussion at regular intervals to determine internal dialogue
EQ 24 But I Didn't Mean . . .	108	4	Medium	Compare and reflect on actual behaviors versus intentions	Worksheet on what said, how interpreted, how to improve result
EQ 25 Trading Spaces	112	4	Low	Compare assertive and nonassertive behaviors and improve empathy for opposite perspective	Trade behavior during a discussion, if normally talkative, be quiet, if normally quiet, be talkative
EQ 26 What Else?	115	4	Low	Uncover unstated opinions or resistance by allowing for thoughtful time and pause before rushing to next agenda	Insert process question "What else" several times until nothing else surfaces in the discussion

Activity	Page Number	7-Step Guide	Level of Risk	Purpose	Quick Synopsis
EQ 27 Channel Surfing	117	4	Low	Determine ways to change the future by imagining new endings to familiar situations	Recall routine situations, then imagine new endings
EQ 28 Voices in Harmony	120	4	Medium	Create ideas/ strategies to overcome negative "voices"	Look for others with same voice—get advice on how to mitigate
EQ 29 Color My World	123	5	Low-Medium	Reflect on emotion in the workplace—learn from past experience	Select a color from fishbowl, assign emotion to color, ask members to reflect on past event
EQ 30 And Now a Word from Our Sponsor	126	2	Low	Improve awareness of strengths and uniqueness	Create a commercial with pictures and verbal component stating strengths
EQ 31 Emotional Trophies	129	5-6	Low	Reinforce connection between intentions and actions in team interactions	Recall positive intentions and actions toward other team members
EQ 32 Secret Admirer	132	1-6	Medium	Build positive relations and learn about strengths	Observer looks for strengths and then gives feedback to person
EQ 33 Accom-plishments Flower Garden	135	1-5-6	Low	Recognize accomplishments and core values and characteristics	Flowers represent accomplishments/ roots represent core values and charac-teristics responsible for success
EQ 34 Profiles in Respect	138	1-5-6	Medium	Recognize and acknowledge characteristics in team members that the team respects	Draw face profile/ have team members write on profile things they respect

(continued)

TABLE 1-1. *(continued)*

Activity	Page Number	7-Step Guide	Level of Risk	Purpose	Quick Synopsis
EQ 35 Perfect Team	140	4	Low	Visualize behaviors of perfect team	Find pictures representing the ideal team and then fix behaviors to the vision
EQ 36 Gut Check	143	1-2	High	Expose team members' feelings about decisions	Place "x" on chart corresponding to feelings about a decision
EQ 37 Timed Reflection	147	5	High	Rate team interaction	Team compares their interaction and determines actions that could improve it
EQ 38 Best Failure	151	5	High	Team members reflect about failure and lessons learned	Team members learn about past behaviors that could have changed outcome
EQ 39 First Impression	154	1-5	Medium	Gain feedback about first impression	Team members tell each other about first impression they had of each other
EQ 40 I Think; I Feel	157	4	Medium	Distinguish between thoughts and feelings in decision making	Team members write thoughts/feelings as they relate to decisions or problem solving
EQ 41 Cartoon Characters	160	1-2	Low	Improve self-awareness and disclose characteristics to team members by using cartoon characters	Team members think about cartoon characters that describe them
EQ 42 Throwing Rocks	163	2-5	Medium	Identify and eliminate traits that are holding team members back	Write words on rocks representing negative characteristics or thought patterns and throw them away

Activity	Page Number	7-Step Guide	Level of Risk	Purpose	Quick Synopsis
EQ 43 The Pause Button	166	3-4	Low	Pause and consider intention before acting	Team members practice PAUSE and use worksheet to predict outcome to various responses
EQ 44 The Pause Elf	170	3	Medium	Help teammates identify warning signs that may be present that may precede negative behavior	Each team member is assigned a Pause Elf to help him/her recognize the warning signs indicating a need for pause
EQ 45 Best Practices	173	6	Low	Help team recognize and celebrate best practices	Brainstorm best practices, reflect on qualities, find ways to celebrate or commemorate
EQ 46 Heroes	176	6	Low	Celebrate qualities in self that imitate heroes	Select heroes and identify qualities in heroes that team members possess
EQ 47 It's in the Air	178	3	Low	Learn and practice a breathing technique to help team pause negative emotional reactions	Practice the steps of deep breathing to pause negative reactions
EQ 48 My Mantra	180	3	Low	Participants identify a mantra to help team shift thinking	Identify a mantra and write the mantra on index cards
EQ 49 Flying Values	183	1-2-6	High	Team members identify when values have been compromised	Write values on paper airplanes to symbolize values "crashes"

(continued)

TABLE 1-1. *(continued)*

Activity	Page Number	7–Step Guide	Level of Risk	Purpose	Quick Synopsis
EQ 50 What's Different?	186	1-2	Medium	Participants identify changes in their lives	Participants bring an old photo and discuss how they were different than they are today

CHAPTER 2

WHAT YOU'LL SEE FOR EACH ACTIVITY

To simplify your choice and help you effectively implement the activities, the descriptions of the activities are consistently divided into the following categories. Not all activities contain all of these categories. For example, if an activity does not have any variations or any cautions, these categories will not appear.

Level of Risk

Each activity is marked as "Low, Medium, or High" to designate its level of risk. By level of risk, we are referring to the level of disclosure that is involved in the activity. Some activities require very little self-disclosure; others require much more. Of course, the more disclosure, the greater the risk for some individuals. It is recommended that the leader or facilitator begin with activities that are low in risk and require little self-disclosure. Once the level of trust of the team increases, the leader can introduce activities that are higher in risk. Although each team is different, the level of difficulty is gauged based on our experience with most groups. Of course, the leader will need to use discretion to determine the comfort level of his or her group. However, just because something might be difficult to address does not mean it should be avoided. Some of the most fruitful activities may be when participants are asked to address difficult topics such as team conflict. It will be important for the leader/facilitator to feel comfortable with the discussion and to create a safe environment for such topics to be addressed.

Purpose

The purpose states what the activity is intended to achieve. It helps the leader/facilitator decide if the activity is the best activity to achieve the desired objective. It gives a brief understanding of the basic concept that the activity is designed to teach. Once the activity is selected, the leader/facilitator should state the purpose to the team, so the team understands what the objective is.

Why Is This Important?

To help the facilitator connect the main concepts of the activity to the team's functioning, this section explains why the concept is important. This information should be used in introducing the activity to the team. Understanding why an activity is useful is very important to people. It serves to give the group the big picture. Adults are much more likely to engage in the learning if they understand why it is important. So, take the time to explain this step.

When to Use This Activity

Each activity includes some suggestions that will help the leader/facilitator determine if the activity is useful for his or her team. It may also give the leader/facilitator new ways to think about the interaction skills of his or her team.

Set the Stage

The leader will be required to introduce each activity to the team. During this period, the leader/facilitator must explain the purpose of the activity and why the concept is important. The leader/facilitator may also be required to explain the concept in a little more depth or provide examples of how the concept relates to work. Sometimes, setting the stage requires the leader to ask a thought provoking question; other times, it requires some simple explanation of a concept or terminology. This step is important in preparing the team for the learning activity, and will help frame the activity for the group so that the maximum learning can occur. For more background information, *The EQ Difference* should be consulted.

Materials

This section lists materials that will be needed to successfully execute the activity. Most activities require no materials or simple materials that are readily available. If a handout is required, it is provided at the end of the activity. It's always useful to have a flip chart and markers handy. Also, it is assumed that the team will be seated at a table.

The Activity

This section gives a step-by-step description of the activity for the leader/facilitator. It explains what the leader should do to conduct the activity.

Key Questions

The key questions are essential for the success of the activity, as they will facilitate learning. They also link the learning to the job, thereby making the learning practical. It is important that the leader/facilitator focus on this debrief period to have a successful outcome. Although we've captured some of the important debrief questions, the leader/facilitator may want to add questions that would be relevant, based on the group and the discussion. For more information on using the key questions, please refer to the section "How to Use This Book—After the Activity" in Chapter 3.

A Word of Caution

This section gives useful advice to the leader/facilitator regarding how to avoid specific problems when facilitating the activity. It gives the leader/facilitator a "heads up" on what can go wrong and what to do about it before it becomes a problem. Also contained in this section are some cautions about when the activity may not be successful. This section is based on the experience of other leaders and facilitators who have used the activity and could be very useful, especially to a novice facilitator.

Variation

Many of the activities in this book can be altered slightly depending on the team's situation. This section contains some suggested variations that could be useful. These variations are based on the experience of other facilitators and leaders. Deviating too far from the activity may not produce the desired outcome, so unless you are an experienced facilitator, we do not recommend too much variation.

Ask for Commitment

The leader/facilitator should ask the team members what they are willing to do back on the job with the information that was gained from the activity. It's important that the facilitator keep the goal in mind, as the goal of this entire book is to improve team interactions on the job. By asking, after each activity, what commitment people are willing to make, the leader/facilitator keeps the group focused on the importance of teamwork and how everyone's actions can contribute to improved teamwork.

CHAPTER 3

HOW TO USE THIS BOOK

Before the Activity

Every activity is different. Every team is different. Every team leader is different. As the team leader/facilitator, it is important that you are well prepared and take into consideration your team, your location, and your team's interests, challenges, quirks, and so on. There is no pat answer to selecting the correct activity. There are no scripts to tell you exactly what to say or what examples to use. Because you know your team better than anyone else, you're the person who knows best what will work. However, by following just a few steps and having a willingness to improve, and an interest in improving, you can definitely successfully facilitate these activities. Here are some ideas to help you prepare before the activity.

1. Think about your team. What are its current challenges? What do you wish to accomplish with an activity? Do you want to broaden the team members' awareness of their impact on one another? Are you trying to get team members to appreciate one another? Are your team members familiar with each other or are they strangers? Is your team experiencing conflict? Are some members dominating? The activities in this book are designed to address a variety of issues depending on the challenge your team is currently experiencing.
2. Select an activity. Use Chapter 1, "A Guide to the 50 Activities," as a starting point. Then read the activity to see if it fits your objective. As the facilitator, you should select activities that you think will work best with your team. The activity you select will depend on many factors, including how long your team has been together,

the personalities of your team members, and what types of issues your team is currently addressing. Although you may want to begin with activities that you know your team would enjoy, stretching and using more challenging activities that involve greater risk is also encouraged.

3. Read the activity several times. Make sure you can visualize the activity as you read it. You should be well prepared. Nothing kills an activity like a leader who doesn't know or understand how the activity is supposed to work. Be sure you can anticipate what's supposed to happen.

4. Think about how you will present the activity and about any personal examples you may wish to use to make the activity relevant. Be sure to include the information in the "Purpose," "Why Is This Important?," and "Setting the Stage" categories in the activity write-up. When using personal examples, **never** point out problems among team members as an example of why this activity is important or what the activity can accomplish. Instead, talk about your personal learning or vulnerability related to the concept. If you expect team members to be candid and learn to improve their self-awareness, you need to speak about yourself as a "work in progress."

5. Think about your role in the activity. What role will the activity require of you? Will you be a coach, a timekeeper, an enforcer? Be prepared to play the role that is required to make the exercise a success. Think about what you will say and how you will sound to properly facilitate the exercise.

6. Gather materials. Most of these activities require few or no materials. However, it will be necessary for you to prepare in advance any materials that will be used for the activities. Prepare handouts ahead of time, and be sure that you have enough for all team members.

7. Set up the room. How will the chairs be arranged? Will you need a flip chart? If the instructions are lengthy, save time and confusion by writing them on the flip chart before the meeting.

8. Think about how you will address potential problems. Every team is different. You know the unique personalities of your team mem-

bers. As you visualize the activity, ask yourself, "What could go wrong?" Prepare to address any problems. Each activity includes a section called "A Word of Caution." Carefully read this section and determine what you could do to prevent problems.

During the Activity

Your role during the activity is that of facilitator. You should not judge the participants or be critical of people's learning; you should facilitate their learning. To help people learn during the activity, consider these suggestions.

1. Don't underestimate the power of your words. How you introduce and position the activity will have much to do with the activity's success. Clearly set the stage for each activity, as the setting gives the team a context within which to experience the activity. That context will help the team learn and accomplish the objective. Be up front about the objective (unless you are instructed not to in the activity write-up.) Tell the group why it is important. Give examples to support it.
2. Always be aware that you are communicating more than your words. Are you enthused about the activity? Are you tentative? Whatever your mood, the group will interpret it, and the success of the activity may hang on your feelings toward the activity.
3. Give clear instructions. If necessary, write the instructions on a flip chart.
4. Check to determine if the group members understand the exercise. After you have explained the activity, ask, "What questions do you have?"
5. During the activity, be sure to be in "facilitator mode." If you are required to be an enforcer, a timekeeper, or play some other role, make sure you do so.
6. Be attentive to the verbal and nonverbal behavior of the group. Watch as the activity unfolds. Note your observations. The observations may be useful during the debrief period after the exercise.
7. If necessary and appropriate for the activity, correct any misunderstandings about the instructions. Do so in a way that does not

place blame. Simply say, "I may not have communicated clearly. Please let me restate the instructions."

8. Respect a person's right to protect himself/herself. If someone feels that the exercise makes him too vulnerable, don't force him to participate.
9. If during the exercise, someone on the team makes an inappropriate comment, redirect it immediately and ask that the group approach conversation in an honorable and respectful way.
10. If things don't go as planned even after you've made attempts to clarify, generally it's best to let it go. You may find that some valuable information comes up during the debrief that could contribute to the learning. As the facilitator, it's best that you remain flexible.

After the Activity

The key questions are used to debrief the activity are the most important part of the exercise. Generally, it is during the debrief period that learning actually takes place. The best way to think about the debrief period is that it is reflective time to generate learning. It is also a fantastic time to learn from one another because everyone sees and experiences things differently.

1. Prepare the group for the debrief period by asking the members to reflect on the process. Encourage the members to reflect on their own learning, as well as be curious about what others experienced.
2. Ask the key questions listed in the activity. Please add additional questions based on your own experience and your understanding of your group's special interests or concerns.
3. Thank people for their comments. Because the debrief is the portion of the exercise that helps people internalize the learning and apply the concepts to the job, be generous and sincere with your appreciation of people's comments.
4. Encourage all members to comment. Recognize that some people will be more forthcoming with comments and others will be more reticent. State early and often that all comments are welcomed and that it's very useful to hear from all members of the group because different points of view are gained.

5. If one person is dominating the discussion, thank the person and say, "What do others think about Joe's comment?"

6. Allow a few moments of silence after you ask a question. One of the mistakes that facilitators make is to fill the silence. By filling the silence, you are essentially telling the group that you will do the talking and the responsibility for them to share their thoughts is taken away.

7. When someone gives an answer, take on the role of facilitator, not judge. A facilitator will ask for clarity, ask for agreement or disagreement, ask people to elaborate, ask people to give examples, and so on. A judge would tell people that they are right or wrong. Avoid this behavior, as it will shut down communication.

CHAPTER 4

FOR THE LEADER

Your Mindset/Role Model

First, as the team leader, you must have the mindset that your team members want to further their understanding about issues that affect the team. You can be most effective as facilitator if you appeal to people's ideals. Most people believe, and will articulate, that they have the best interests of the team in mind. However, sometimes one's daily behavior doesn't live up to that intention. Your job as the team leader is to help people live up to their best intentions. By appealing to their best intentions, you set the individuals and the team up for a successful and positive experience.

Second, put yourself on an equal level of learning with your team. Even though you are the leader and facilitator and may understand the concepts, understanding the concepts and practicing them in your daily interactions are two different things. So, as the facilitator, you can greatly enhance the effectiveness of these exercises if you point out examples of your own behavior that you are working to understand and improve. Besides, you then become a role model for everyone else, so they can look at their own behavior and seek to improve.

Next, always look for the opportunity to find positive interactions among your team members. These positive interactions are instant opportunities to provide positive feedback to your team. Celebrate your team's successful interactions, as described later in this chapter.

Also, remember that no one is perfect. We all have bad days, lapses of manners, and emotionally unintelligent moments. The objective is to use this information to build better teamwork and interaction skills. Your team members will undoubtedly make mistakes in their interactions. When these things happen, reinforce the idea of letting it go, granting forgiveness, and moving on. A large part of emotional intelligence is gaining perspective about what's important and what's a waste of energy. Coach people to stay focused on getting the work done as a team and how part of that requires us to recognize that our teammates are human.

The least effective thing you can do is to use this information to label people. Be sure to set the tone early and often that respectful and honorable relationships are the goal and that the information learned in the activities should be used to support that goal, not point out people's faults.

Also, recognize your role as a coach. Coaching helps people retain learning and change their behavior on the job. As long as you come across as a sincere and humble fellow learner, your efforts to coach can transform the workplace. The least effective impact would be for you to come across in an arrogant way—that somehow you know all about emotional intelligence and that you have all the answers. In fact, much of what you'll do as a coach is ask the right questions. Here are some ideas that will help you in your role as coach.

1. Help people identify their intentions. Keep people focused by asking, "What are your intentions regarding your interactions with your teammates?"

2. Help people set goals for their behavior. Ask, "What would you like to see yourself do more of . . . ? Less of . . . ?"

3. KEEP PEOPLE FOCUSED ON THE WORK GOALS. Ask, "What can you do that will help our team get the work out on time? What can you do that will help our team make fewer errors? What can you do that will help our team better serve the customer?"

4. When someone comes to you with a problem, ask, "What do you think would work?"

5. Ask, "What have we talked about in our team meetings (activities) that we might be able to apply here?"

6. Also, in terms of emotional intelligence and team interactions, you should almost always direct the person back to the team member that he or she is having a problem with. Ask, "Have you talked to Sam about this situation?" I say almost always because if the employee brings a concern about harassment, violence, or

some other problem of a very serious nature, you may have to intervene.

Learn More

Because the exercises in this book are based on *The EQ Difference: A Powerful Plan for Putting Emotional Intelligence to Work,* it is important that you learn more about the seven steps. It is highly recommended that you use *The EQ Difference* as a basic resource because the steps and the language are consistent with the activities presented here. In fact, that book is written for anyone in the workplace interested in improving emotional intelligence, so it would be appropriate to make copies available for your team if they are interested in learning more. Some departments are reading the book along with performing the exercises. The concepts of emotional intelligence are extremely useful at work and at home, so people are generally very interested in learning more. Some people enjoy reading and others don't, so use your judgment and give people a choice. There are also additional resources named in the back of this book for those who want to learn more.

Reinforce Behaviors

The most powerful thing you can do as the leader is to reinforce the application of learning from the activities when the team members return to the job. Your involvement as the facilitator puts you in a strong position to coach and remind people about what they learned. Every activity in this book contributes to learning that can improve teamwork and interaction skills. Here are some suggestions for reinforcing the lessons learned from the activities.

1. First, look for opportunities to find people doing the correct things and positively reinforce their behavior. Catch people doing positive things and say something specific about them. Infusing the environment with positive feedback is contagious and will reinforce the kind of team environment that you desire.

2. Remember what people say during the debrief period following each activity. When something comes up on the job, restate their comments. Do this in a manner that makes the person the hero; do not say anything in a punitive way. Noticing and remembering what the person said is also very affirming. It is a way of honoring

their participation in the activity. Then, you further honor their positive behavior back on the job.

3. If your team is having a problem on the job, ask the members to relate the job situation to one of the activities. Based on what they learned about teamwork and emotional intelligence, ask for their opinion about how to solve the problem. This technique reinforces the concepts, but it also does something else; it teaches them to solve their own problems and rely on their own expertise and intentions to act positively for the good of the team.

4. Suggest that the team members keep a journal of lessons learned. Logging the lessons adds another layer of reinforcement to the learning. Not everyone is going to want to keep a journal, but for some it will be an enjoyable and useful learning tool. One team kept a team journal. At the end of each meeting, the team decided on one "gem" and logged it in the journal. Another team used a "quotes" journal to track its learning. After each meeting, the members found a quotation that represented something of value they learned from the meeting.

5. Once your team begins to excel, use the members to help other teams in your organization. In one organization, teams mentored other teams. Team members talked about how to get beyond differences to accomplish goals. They became the biggest advocates for teamwork because they had overcome some very difficult situations.

6. Always look for avenues to showcase your team's accomplishments. By accomplishments, I'm referring to productivity and quality measures. Then, have your team members talk about how they achieved such good results.

7. Look for posters, quotations or other items that reinforce the lessons discussed in the activities. Also, look for visual reminders to display. Connecting the lessons to something visual will help people's minds create a lasting impression of the lesson.

8. Rotate responsibility of team members to self-monitor the group for positive interactions that contribute to production or quality improvement. Ask the team to self-report positive interactions.

9. Visible celebrations are important to reinforce concepts. The celebrations need not be elaborate. They do, however, need to be tied

to something specific. What are you celebrating? Why is it important to the team interactions? How does that lead to improved productivity, quality, or customer service?

10. Let others know about what your team has accomplished. Invite company leaders to visit your team. Arrange for a "round table" where your team is the featured attraction. Let the members talk about what they have been learning and how it's good for the company. Make them heroes.

Timing and Readiness

Some managers who pick up this book will do so because they know their team is ready and willing to improve their interaction skills. Others, who have a seriously dysfunctional team member may be grasping at straws and looking for answers when other measures are required. No activity is going to turn around a seriously dysfunctional person. This is not about therapy; it's about teamwork and gaining awareness about basic team interactions and their impact so that improvements can be made. If you're looking for an answer to a seriously troubled employee, this probably isn't the right approach.

However, most people are open to the ideas in this book. They will recognize the usefulness of the concepts and realize they can apply them both at home and on the job. As the leader, begin with low-risk activities and determine how the group responded to them. Also, some of the activities are designed to celebrate the team's strengths. Use these activities first to promote the positive nature of the learning. Then, gradually introduce activities that require people to look at negative interactions.

As Your Team Develops

Your team may already be self-directed. If so, it would probably welcome the idea that one of the members, rather than you, take responsibility for selecting and facilitating some activities. In fact, your job may be as simple as handing the members this book as a resource and then participating as they see fit. If your team isn't accustomed to this type of independence, you may begin to lead the team in this direction. After some initial successful activities facilitated by you, you may ask the members if they would be interested in taking responsibility for the activities.

What If . . .

Sometimes, as the leader or facilitator, you could be thinking the worst. You could be thinking . . . what if things go wrong? what if no one participates? what if no one answers the key questions? Well, things could go wrong. People could choose not to participate, and people may not be able to answer the key questions. So what advice do we have?

First, don't let it rattle you. We'll give you some advice on how to handle different situations, but the overriding advice is that the team leader should be careful not to overreact. If you feel that something is a disaster, your team will pick up your stress. Your attitude should be one of fun and learning, as your attitude goes a long way toward averting some of the problems. So, remember that attitude can be helpful even in the event that things don't go as planned.

WHAT IF THINGS GO WRONG?

Remember that it's possible no one knows the activity didn't go as planned. If that's the case, just go ahead and debrief the activity as it occurred. You may find that you created an interesting variation of the exercise. If people do notice that something didn't go as planned, just admit it. By being up front about it, you demonstrate candid and open behavior. Discuss it with the group, and you may learn something that you can apply to the next activity.

WHAT IF NO ONE PARTICIPATES?

Well, that will put a fizzle in your day. But again, be candid. Tell the group that you had hoped people would find the exercise useful. Ask the members to help you understand why they didn't want to participate. If this happens, your team may have some important issues to discuss. Be open. Listen to their comments. Don't pass judgment. Frankly, it would be very unusual for the entire group to choose not to participate. If one person doesn't participate, ask him or her to help in some other way. It is also effective to let the other group members address this issue. Just be sure that the team keeps it honorable.

WHAT IF NO ONE ANSWERS THE KEY QUESTIONS?

As the facilitator, one of your most important techniques is silence. Ask the question, and then just wait. More than likely, someone will answer it. Make eye contact with the group as you ask the question and during the silence. If no one comes forward, you can make a statement and ask the group to use a show of hands to determine if they agree with your answer. By asking people to raise their hands, you are gaining their participation. Then, you can follow up by asking, "Why do you agree or disagree with the statement?"

WHAT IF THE "GROUP THINK" TURNS ON YOU?

Occasionally, someone in the group may jump to a negative conclusion. For example, someone might say something like, "I don't think we should help team members if they don't help us. I think we should make them suffer." The group may surprise you by joining in and agreeing with the statement. Your role will be to challenge the group to think about the consequences to the customer. It will also be useful to ask how that will affect teamwork in the future. In addition, you'll want to explore reasons why the person may not be offering assistance, or other ways to confront the person who isn't offering assistance.

Conclusion

Overall, as the leader/facilitator, it's important that you are comfortable with the concepts of emotional intelligence and that you are a willing learner. If you approach EQ from the point of view that you are going to "teach" this to someone, then you may come across as arrogant. Learn with the group. Share your own insights, your struggles and challenges, your failures and your mistakes. This will allow the team members to see you in a way that makes you real. As you share your vulnerabilities, you are building an open trusting relationship with your team members, and their respect for you grows deeper.

CHAPTER 5

THE ACTIVITIES

EQ 1 Mood Check

Level of Risk

Low

Purpose

This exercise is designed to help each team member understand his or her mood, as well as identify the moods of others on the team. It also helps team members to be candid about feelings, which can lead to building trust and openness.

Why Is This Important?

Moods of team members will impact the performance of the team. Why? Because (1). moods are contagious, (2). moods affect how people relate to one another, and (3). moods affect the decision-making and energy of the team.

When to Use This Activity

This exercise is great to use at the start of a team meeting to gauge the feelings of the members and to set the stage for members to express and reveal themselves by creating an open and honest culture. It's also useful when new team members join a team, as it allows them to gain a better understanding of their teammates.

Set the Stage

Ask the group, "Have you ever experienced a time when you were in a great mood and were able to fly through a stack of work? Or maybe the opposite, you were feeling low and accomplishing even the simplest task seemed overwhelming?" Ask team members to draw on their personal experiences to think about how mood can affect performance.

Materials

The Six Families of Emotion Chart (see Handout 5-1).
Colored sticky dots.

The Activity

1. Duplicate the Six Families of Emotion chart (Handout 5-1) and place it in a visible location. This can be done in a number of different ways, such as duplicating it on a large piece of poster board that can be reused, writing it on flip chart paper, and projecting it on a screen or wall using an LCD projector. It should be visible to all members of the team.
2. Give each team member a colored sticky dot.
3. Ask each team member to place the dot on the chart to indicate his or her present emotion.

Key Questions

- As we look at where people have placed their dots, what patterns do we see?
- How might people's moods affect our meeting today?
- How can moods affect our energy toward team goals?
- How can moods affect our decision making as a team?
- What can you tell us about mood and performance?
- Are we always aware of our moods? How can we increase our awareness of our moods?

- Are we stuck with our moods?
- What power do we have over our moods?
- What can you do to change your mood?

Ask for Commitment

At the end of the meeting, ask, "How might you be willing to use what we discussed today in your daily work?"

HANDOUT 5-1 The Six Families of Emotion

Happy	Depressed	Surprised	Anxious	Angry	Creative
Content	Sad	Shocked	Fearful	Enraged	Imaginative
Ecstatic	Suicidal	Dumbfounded	Worried	Sarcastic	Resourceful
Joyous	Melancholy	Startled	Concerned	Annoyed	Artistic
Pleased	Grieving	Astonished	Nervous	Furious	Inspired
Cheerful	Gloomy	Amazed	Uneasy	Irritated	Innovative
Blissful	Miserable	Stunned	Restless	Irate	Ingenious
Exultant	Heartbroken	Flabbergasted	Fretful	Livid	Inquisitive
Delighted	Distressed	Astounded	Frightened	Incensed	Playful
Jovial	Apathetic	Taken Aback	Panicky	Cross	Pioneering

EQ 2 I Can Top That

Level of Risk

Medium

Purpose

This exercise examines the negative nature of competition in pursuit of attention, power, and ego. It will help team members understand that when we compete for attention, it takes attention away from others and from the group's goals.

Why Is This Important?

In a healthy team environment, members should focus on the team goals and what's good for the group. Competition in a team environment always puts the focus on the individual rather than the team. If team members focus on getting their ideas accepted, winning others over to their positions, or finding fault with the ideas of others, all of their energy and focus is on themselves and not on the team's goals. Also, it hampers true listening because the team member only listens to find agreement with his or her position or to argue a point made by another member.

When to Use This Activity

Use this exercise when team members are not fully aware of the impact of how they come across with their ideas. Also, use it to sensitize team members to the idea that presenting ideas or solutions in a team isn't about one person "winning."

Set the Stage

Ask the group the following, "Have you ever been in a situation where no matter what you say, someone else chimes in and lets you know about their similar experience. But somehow, their experience is bigger, better, more dramatic, more important, or somehow more superlative?" Give an example.

Materials

Flip chart and marker.

The Activity

1. Select a fun subject that appeals to all team members. For example, if all the teammates happen to be parents, you might decide to select the topic of children. If you can't think of one subject that will appeal to everyone, separate the team into two or more smaller groups and select separate topics for each group.
2. Let's assume you've selected children as the topic. Instruct the group to think about some of the cutest things their children have ever done. Give the group a couple of minutes to think about their examples.
3. Ask a group member to start by relaying a story about his or her child. Then, instruct the group members to genuinely listen long enough to understand what the story is about, but then interrupt the story with the opening statement, "**That's nothing, let me tell you about my son/daughter . . .**" The objective is to continue to top what the other person is saying. All parties should be involved in topping or competing to tell the "best" story.
4. Continue this until all members have tried to top each other's stories and the interaction becomes chaotic and spontaneous.

Some Suggested Topics for Stories

Best participation in sports
Best/most unusual vacation
Best/most unusual things you received as birthday gifts
Best pets
Worst medical experiences
Worst accidents
Worst in-laws
Worst dates
Worst job/boss

Key Questions

- What words would you use to describe this conversation? *(Although the conversation might be funny, look for words such as competitive, put down, rude, and better than.)*
- When you were participating in this conversation, what were you thinking about?
- What feeling does the opening line, "That's nothing, . . ." create? *(It's a put down and it also steals the focus from the speaker.)*
- What happens to listening skills in a conversation like this?
- If this behavior occurs in a team meeting or workplace when we're trying to solve a problem or generate ideas, what would be the effect on the team?
- Do you think that people are always aware of their impact on others?
- What can we do to increase our awareness?
- How do you think you should approach someone who treats you like this?

A Word of Caution

Be sure people do not use people's names in their stories. For example, if they are talking about their worst boss, ask that they not name names. It could be another manager in your company, and your objective isn't to talk about others.

Variation

You can list the topics on the flip chart and ask the team members to select the topic they would like to use.

Ask for Commitment

At the end of the meeting, ask, "How might you be willing to use what we discussed today in your daily work?"

EQ 3 Lead Balloons

Level of Risk

High

Purpose

The purpose of this activity is to help the team discover areas of unresolved conflict or discord that drains the team's energy or shuts down team communication. This exercise will help team members recognize, talk about, and name the conflict that is affecting the team's performance.

Why Is This Important?

Resolving conflict is essential in any team. You can't resolve conflict unless you recognize that conflict exists. This exercise is an excellent way to open the door to conflict recognition and, ultimately, resolution. It gives visual form to what the group is experiencing. If conflict is left unresolved, it can drain the energy, creativity, communication, and productivity of the team.

When to Use This Activity

Use this activity after (or during) a difficult team meeting where team members became silent or ideas were just dropped because of opposition or resistance. This can be used as an opening to process the dynamics behind silence, opposition, or resistance.

Set the Stage

The facilitator can prepare the group by saying "You've all heard the expression, 'It went over like a lead balloon.' What do you think that means?" Ask the group members to give their opinions on the meaning of the expression. Then, the facilitator can continue with, "Yesterday at our team meeting, I observed a lead balloon during our discussion."

Materials

A balloon filled with graphite, beans, lentils or other matter.
Flip chart and marker.

The Activity

1. Drop a lead balloon in the center of the meeting table.
2. Ask each team member to think about yesterday's interaction and identify the possible causes of the lead balloon. Instruct the team members to think analytically, and not emotionally, about the discussion. Give the team members examples of this. Don't allow them to say, "Joe is unreasonable." Instruct them to comment on the issue, not the person.
3. Write the ideas or possible causes on the flip chart. Be sure to ask everyone's opinion. As the facilitator, be sure to keep the group members thinking and speaking analytically and avoiding personal attacks.
4. Process the key questions with the group. Afterwards, assist the group in resolving the conflict.

Key Questions

- ➤ What impact do lead balloons have on our team's interaction?
- ➤ If we ignore the lead balloon, do you think it will go away?
- ➤ Why do you think we have a tendency to ignore lead balloons?
- ➤ What would make it easier to face our lead balloons?
- ➤ What can we learn from facing lead balloons?
- ➤ How can we benefit from facing lead balloons?

A Word of Caution

This exercise is not for the faint of heart. The purpose is to get the group to recognize that a conflict exists. From here, it's up to the skilled facilitator to help the group address the conflict and any negative group dynamics. By all means, you must ensure that all group members are heard and their opinions are respected.

Variation

Fill some balloons with graphite, beans, lentils or some other substance and keep them visible during future team meetings. When the team starts to lose energy or go silent because of discord or unresolved conflict, ask team members to pick up a "lead balloon" and toss it in the center of the table. This enables the team to recognize the issue and spend time resolving it, rather than pretending it doesn't exist. It also helps team members become accountable for recognizing conflict and discord in the team and talking about it rather than letting it fester.

Ask for Commitment

At the end of the meeting, ask, "What are we willing to commit to that would change the way our team addresses conflict?"

EQ 4 When Things Go Wrong—Our Team M.O.

Level of Risk

Medium

Purpose

This exercise serves an important purpose by helping team members recognize patterns of behavior that could be interfering with the team's ability to reach its goals. We call these patterns of behavior, M.O.s, or modus operandi. They are predictable patterns of how the team performs under various situations or circumstances.

Why Is This Important?

All groups form patterns in their interactions. In team language, we talk about the stages of a team as forming, storming, norming, and performing. Norming behavior is when the team has established routines. During the norming stage, the team's interactions are on autopilot and people settle into roles. However, sometimes even when teams are functioning well, under certain circumstances, the team's patterns of behavior, or M.O.s, can be improved. It's useful if team members can see their M.O.s, so they can choose the manner in which they interact rather than perform on autopilot.

When to Use This Activity

It is best to use this exercise after a team has been functioning for a while and routines have been established. It would also be useful if a team has a pattern of behavior or M.O. during certain situations that are obviously destructive. This exercise would not be useful in a newly formed team.

Set the Stage

Ask the group to think about a sports team that they follow. Ask them if they can recall the sports commentator's remarks on the team's behaviors. Share some ideas, such as "This team is good under pressure. They are able to deliver results when the going gets tough." Or, "This team tends to fall apart when the pressure is on. They have trouble mustering the strength to get them out of difficult situations." Explain that the team members are going to have an opportunity to be outside commentators on their team's interactions.

The Activity

1. Ask each team member to write some comments as if he/she were an outside narrator commenting on the team's M.O. Give the team the following situations to comment on:

   a. "If you were an outside observer/narrator commenting on your team, what would you say about this team's performance when someone else criticizes it?"
   b. "If you were an outside observer/narrator commenting on your team, what would you say about this team's performance when the team experiences disagreement or conflict?"
   c. "If you were an outside observer/narrator commenting on your team, what would you say about this team's performance when the team has a very heavy workload?"
   d. "If you were an outside observer/narrator commenting on your team, what would you say about this team's performance when the team is under pressure?"
   e. "If you were a outside observer/narrator commenting on your team, what would you say about this team's performance when the team is defeated?"

2. Ask team members to read their comments.

Key Questions

- ➤ Why is it useful to step outside the team and try to become an observer to determine how the team functions?
- ➤ What can we learn when we observe a team's behavior patterns?

- How can being aware of the team's typical behavior patterns lead to improved team performance?
- Do you think that M.O.s apply to individual behavior patterns, as well as to a team's behavior pattern?
- If you are aware of your individual M.O., how can it help you?
- Can we change our team's or our individual M.O.?
- When would we want to change?
- What are some ideas or ways in which we can change M.O.s?

A Word of Caution

It's important that the facilitator keep the discussion focused on the team and the team's function, not individuals within the team. Once the team has reached a high level of trust, it would be useful to discuss individual M.O.s as outlined in the variation below.

Variation

Determine individual M.O.s within the team by having each team member think about what they consider to be their M.O. in the team. After members have identified their individual M.O.s, invite other team members to comment. The level of difficulty will be high for this variation.

Ask for Commitment

At the end of the meeting, ask, "How might you be willing to use what we discussed today in your daily work?"

EQ 5 Helium Balloons

Level of Risk

Medium

Purpose

This exercise is designed to help each team member understand positive interactions and their effects on the team. It will also help develop awareness of positive interactions and encourage such interactions within the team and with other groups. This exercise is very upbeat and is a good energizer for fostering positive feelings among team members.

Why Is This Important?

It's important for team members to receive feedback about their behaviors that have a positive impact on the team. Feedback will reinforce positive behavior and encourage people to continue to find ways to positively impact the team. Also, because the mood of team members is contagious, it is very important for people to understand how they affect each other.

When to Use This Activity

This exercise is great to use at the start of a team meeting to energize the participants. It's a great team building exercise that can help spread positive feeling among team members. It's best to use this exercise after the team has been interacting for some time and is able to give each teammate positive feedback. However, it can also be valuable in the early stages of team development because it sets the stage for members to express positive sentiments about one another and reinforce positive behavior.

Set the Stage

Ask the group the following: "Have you ever been around someone who is energizing? When you are in this person's company, you just feel lighter and that life is easier rather than a burden. It's like you have helium balloons attached to you that just make going through the day easier?" Ask team members to draw on their personal examples to think about how these positive experiences give them a lift.

Materials

Helium balloons: At least one for each team member. If you would like to make a bigger impression, give each team member helium balloons equal to the total number of team members. So, if there are 6 team members, each person would receive 6 balloons.

The Activity

1. The facilitator should start by asking the team to think about one specific team member. Ask the team to describe one thing this member says or does that creates a positive effect for the team.
2. In turn, each teammate should express the positive behavior and give the teammate under discussion a helium balloon. (If the facilitator is using just one balloon per person, then the facilitator should give the person the balloon on behalf of the team after each team member has expressed his/her sentiments.)
3. Then, the facilitator should move on to the next person until all teammates have been presented with a helium balloon.

Key Questions

- Why is it important to know what we do that creates a positive impact on our team?
- What can we do with the information we gained from our teammates today?
- How did it make you feel to hear what your teammates had to say?

A Word of Caution

As the facilitator, please coach and instruct the team that all teammates must say something positive about each teammate. If you happen to have a very negative team member and you don't think the team will have anything positive to say about him or her, this exercise may flop. However, depending on how skilled you are as a facilitator, it could work well to create discussion around team member behavior that is positive and team member behavior that is negative. However, as the facilitator you should understand that the intent would be different when you begin the exercise and you should frame it differently.

Variation

Instead of talking about a specific team member's behaviors, the facilitator can ask the group to come up with the types of behaviors that would constitute a positive experience for the team. In this scenario, the team would be discussing positive behaviors that they think would contribute to a positive team experience. The facilitator could then have the team members pledge to adopt these behaviors as their own. It would be more in line with creating a positive vision of the behaviors that would be positive for the team than specific feedback regarding individual team member's behavior. This would make it a lower risk exercise.

Ask for Commitment

Ask the team to think about things they could do everyday to bring "helium" to the team.

EQ 6 Hair Triggers or Hot Buttons

Level of Risk

High

Purpose

The purpose of this activity is to help team members identify and verbalize some of their triggers or hot buttons. Once triggers are identified and verbalized, other team members can choose to act in a manner that is respectful of others' triggers.

Why Is This Important?

Triggers or hot buttons are events, words, phrases, situations, or a combination of things that create a negative emotional reaction. Our triggers are conditioned by our life experiences, and what constitutes a trigger for one person may have absolutely no affect on someone else. It is important for each of us to be aware of our triggers and then to take steps to deter the triggers from manifesting themselves negatively. Also, in a team environment, it is helpful when teammates can learn about their teammates' triggers and choose to be respectful of those triggers by, if possible, avoiding the events, words, phrases, or situations that upset others.

When to Use This Activity

This activity is useful to increase self-awareness of the group members. It can be used anytime. It can also be used after a conflict situation that was aggravated by a trigger.

Set the Stage

Explain to the group that everyone has certain situations, events, words, or phrases that may set off a negative emotional reaction. The facilitator should give an example of a trigger. For example, if you like things neat and orderly, a trigger might be to enter a messy workspace. Describe how it feels when the trigger presents itself. Explain to the group that awareness of triggers is very useful because we can understand our reaction and also take steps to prevent our reaction from interfering with our performance.

Materials

Unfinished sentences written on a flip chart or worksheet.
A button marked HOT placed in the middle of the meeting table.

The Activity

1. Give the group members some time to think about their triggers or hot buttons. If people need some help, you can ask them to complete the following unfinished sentences:

   a. It makes me angry when . . .
   b. I don't like it when people . . .
   c. I feel offended when . . .
   d. I think it's rude to . . .
   e. At work, I wish people would . . .
   f. At work, I think it would be a better place if people would stop . . .
   g. It makes me crazy when . . .
   h. If people would only . . .
   i. It makes me angry when people say . . .
   j. I get irritated when I come into work and . . .

Key Questions

- Why is it useful to identify our triggers? Our teammates' triggers?
- What steps can we take to overcome our triggers or our emotional reactions to the triggers?
- How can being aware of our teammates' triggers help our team?
- How can being aware of our teammates' triggers improve our interactions?
- What steps can we take to understand our teammates' triggers?
- Under what circumstances are our triggers more likely to be a problem and set off a negative emotional reaction?

A Word of Caution

A very sinister teammate could use the knowledge of people's hot buttons in negative and destructive ways. If you notice this behavior, you will need to discuss it with the team member.

Variation

Use the HOT BUTTON as a visual in the meeting room for future team meetings. It would be useful if the button were hooked up to a buzzer or some other sound. When teammates were treading near someone's trigger, someone could press the HOT BUTTON and the sound could serve as a reminder that the conversation could be rerouted for a more productive interaction.

Ask for Commitment

At the end of the meeting, ask, "How might you be willing to use what we discussed today in your daily work?"

Level of Risk

Low–Medium

Purpose

Everyone has experienced a spirit killer. A spirit killer is a comment that creates a negative drain on the climate of the group. Although spirit killers can take many forms, it is usually a form of verbal violence that causes teammates to experience a decline in energy or enthusiasm for a task or idea. The purpose of this exercise is to increase people's awareness of potential spirit killers, so they can avoid them during team interaction. It is also useful to prepare a team to respond to and distinguish among legitimate questions or concerns regarding the team's ideas from a spirit killer.

Why Is This Important?

Spirit killers drain energy and kill enthusiasm, creativity and productivity. Obviously, energy, enthusiasm, creativity, and productivity are desirable qualities. Acts that diminish these qualities are not good for the team.

When to Use This Activity

This activity is appropriate at many different points during the team's development. You can use this activity early in the team's development to help the members think about ways to interact with one another. You can also use this activity when a team is experiencing a lack of energy or enthusiasm that may be the result of spirit killers. This activity is particularly useful to discuss the difference between spirit killers and legitimate questions or challenges regarding an idea.

Set the Stage

Ask the group members to think about times where they were excited about an idea and someone made a statement to kill their enthusiasm.

Give a personal example to support the idea of a spirit killer. An example might be when you presented a good idea to someone and he or she said, "That will never work." This phrase is a classic spirit killer.

Materials

Flip chart and markers.

The Activity

1. Facilitate a brainstorming session where teammates generate a list of spirit killers. Ask the group to think about several words or phrases that people say that feel like spirit killers.
2. List the phrases on a flip chart.

Key Questions

- What effect do spirit killers have on the team?
- What can you do with this list of spirit killers?
- How can being aware of spirit killers help the team?
- What's the difference between a spirit killer and a legitimate concern?
- Can a legitimate concern or question sometimes seem like a spirit killer?
- What can you do if you have a legitimate concern or question to be sure that it doesn't sound like a spirit killer?
- (If you've already done the exercise on triggers, you might ask the following question.) How are a spirit killer and a trigger similar? Different? (They can be similar if a spirit killer happens to be a trigger for you. They are different, however, because a trigger is your internal hot button. It may cause a negative reaction in you, but have nothing to do with another person. For example, walking into a messy work area can be a trigger for you and yet, other people function and perform just fine.)

A Word of Caution

Be sure the discussion does not become personal. A spirit killer is a behavior, not a person. Keep the group focused on discussion behaviors.

Variation

Give $1 for Your Spirit Killers. Place the list of spirit killers generated from the meeting in a visible location in the team's work area or meeting area. Put a jar in the middle of the team's work area and have each team member contribute $1 for every spirit killer they utter. Later, use the money for a pizza party or some other purpose the team chooses.

Ask for Commitment

Ask the team to keep the brainstormed list visible and add to it when additional spirit killers surface. Also, give the list to new team members to help them understand the potential impact of their words.

UP

Level of Risk

Low

Purpose

The purpose of this activity is to energize the group by getting people up on their feet and using physical movement to activate brain function.

Why Is This Important?

After sitting for long periods of time, or after a heavy lunch, it is important to introduce physical exercise to energize the group. Once the energy returns, the group is ready to focus on the task at hand.

When to Use This Activity

Use this activity after lunch or at another time when the group seems laggard.

Set the Stage

Tell the team members that just when their bodies are telling them they would like to take a nap, you're going to help them do the exact opposite to reenergize the team.

The Activity

1. Ask the group to stand up and form a circle.
2. Ask each member to think about a simple body movement, such as a clap, a kick, a twist, and so on.
3. Beginning with one member of the circle, have the member introduce his or her activity.
4. Ask all group members to repeat the movement.

5. Then, ask the second member of the circle to introduce another movement.
6. Ask the group to repeat the first movement, followed by the second.
7. Repeat this until all members of the circle have introduced a movement and the group repeats all of the movements introduced by each member.
8. As the facilitator, you should ask the group to repeat the entire process if they make a mistake. Set the tempo to perform the movements quickly. At the end, ask the group to repeat the movements several times and at a quicker pace. End with a round of applause.

Key Questions

- How does movement change us?
- How can we use movement in the course of our teamwork?
- What does movement do for stress?

A Word of Caution

If your team has more than eight members, you may want to break the group into two teams, because it is hard to remember more than eight movements at a time.

If you have someone who is unable to participate because of physical limitations, you can make that person an observer to help the facilitator check the group for mistakes. Be sensitive to the person to determine if this is an acceptable role. You know your team members, so use your judgment.

Variation

The facilitator can introduce all of the movements. In that way, the facilitator can practice the movements, keep the group on track, and ask them to repeat if they forget something.

EQ 9 Strung Tight—Understanding M.O.s During High Stress

Level of Risk

High

Purpose

The purpose of this activity is to help team members identify their M.O., as it relates to stress. Individual M.O.s, or patterns of behavior, affect individual, as well as team performance. By understanding our patterns of behavior under certain high stress situations, we are better prepared to adjust negative behavior and channel our stress in a more productive way.

Why Is This Important?

Most people experience stress on their jobs to some degree or another. High stress could result from demanding customers, a heavy workload, or when things at home are not going very well. Most people have predictable patterns of dealing with stress. For some, it might be to work harder and at a more frenetic pace; others may find it difficult to focus on the task; still others might choose to overeat or to lash out at others. The point is that we typically revert to established patterns of behavior when we feel stressed. If we become aware of these patterns, we can choose to react in a healthier manner. Without awareness, we are doomed to repeat negative patterns.

When to Use This Activity

This activity can be useful at any time. In particular, if you notice that the team is experiencing high stress, use this activity to help members understand their reactions to high stress and discuss alternative behaviors that may have a more positive effect for the individual and the team. Also, use it to open the discussion about process improvements that can be made to eliminate stress in the workload.

Set the Stage

Explain to the group that most people experience stress to some degree or another. Explain that stress could be fueled by many different sources. When possible, it is certainly best to eliminate the source of stress, but sometimes that is simply impossible. The next best thing is to understand our reaction to the stress and do something positive to eliminate the stress reaction.

Materials

Notepads and pencils.

The Activity

1. Ask the group members to think about times when they felt particularly stressed. Ask them to recall these times and to try to picture how they reacted to stress. Allow the group to think silently about this for a few minutes.
2. Give members a notepad and pencil, and ask them to jot down their self-observations.
3. After the group has had some time to think, ask members to describe how they act when they are feeling stressed.
4. Ask other group members to give feedback concurring or disputing the group member's observation about his or her behavior under stress.

Key Questions

- Why is it useful to be aware of our M.O. when we are experiencing high stress?
- Is it possible to change our pattern of reaction to stress?
- Is it possible to avoid stress?
- If it is possible to eliminate the source of the stress, why is that a better solution than trying to cope with it?
- How much of stress is related to how we think about a particular situation versus the actual situation?

- ➤ What are some positive behaviors or thoughts that work to alleviate stress?
- ➤ Do you think it is possible to replace negative M.O.s with positive M.O.s?
- ➤ How does our reaction to stress affect the rest of the team?
- ➤ What can we do to help one another during a stressful period?
- ➤ Are there things within our work environment that we could do to eliminate the source of stress? If so, let's discuss them.

A Word of Caution

Do not use this activity as a substitute for a good process or good leadership. If something in the work environment is contributing to stress that could be corrected by improving a process or by providing other tools or direction, by all means do so. For example, one company had a particularly busy workload at the end of the day. As a result, team members worked overtime, missing family dinners and soccer practice. The reason for the end of the day rush, however, was easily corrected by changing the mail pick up time. So, don't try to substitute stress management for good process improvements.

Variation

If you have a cohesive team whose members respect one another's opinions, it would be very useful for teammates to give feedback about each other's M.O. You could begin by asking for a volunteer to go first. Then, encourage teammates to offer feedback about what they observed when this person is in high-stress situations. Coach the volunteer to just listen and say thank you after each person's comment. This is a great 360 feedback session without the paperwork. You can also ask team members to give the volunteer "advice" regarding alternative behaviors he or she may wish to consider when experiencing high stress. After the first volunteer, ask for another volunteer. (You can also be the first to volunteer to "set the stage.")

Ask for Commitment

At the end of the meeting, ask, "How might you be willing to use what we discussed today in your daily work?"

EQ 10 Team Trophies

Level of Risk

Low

Purpose

The Purpose of this exercise is for team members to recognize when things are going well and to celebrate the team's accomplishments.

Why Is This Important?

Celebrating the team's accomplishments serves several purposes. It reinforces positive behavior. It encourages positive feelings about the team and team members. It creates a positive climate and sets a climate that is focused on achievement. It helps team members get in the habit of focusing on the positive rather than negative attributes of the team.

When to Use This Activity

This activity has such merit that it should be a regular feature within the framework of your team's activities. Once a month or so, the team should focus on its accomplishments, quantify them, and celebrate them. If, however, team production or quality is poor, this activity can be used to encourage team members to discuss what they could do to accomplish more trophies.

Set the Stage

Every team has good and bad days. However, sometimes we don't stop and acknowledge our accomplishments. Today, let's reflect on our accomplishments and celebrate them.

Materials

Two flip charts and markers.

Trophies—all shapes and sizes. To minimize expense, you can use pictures of trophies or some other symbol printed on cardstock.

Because the trophy is just a symbol, anything works as long as the group understands the significance of the object. One company used bananas, because the CEO walked by and heard about a particular accomplishment and reached for the first thing he could get his hands on, which happened to be a banana. Another company uses fake paper dollars that have the picture of the CEO on them. Still another company uses toy building blocks because the company sees the significance of each act as a building block to a better company.

The Activity

1. At a regular interval (once a month, once a quarter, or whatever is appropriate for your team), ask the members to brainstorm a list of accomplishments. Instruct the team to think about accomplishments on two levels:

   a. Accomplishments that improve quality, productivity, or costs for the overall good of the business or organization.

   b. Accomplishments that relate to how we get the job done. These items are related to the way the team lives the values, how they interact with one another, and how team members respond to difficult situations.

2. Write the accomplishments on two flip charts, separating the accomplishments according to the categories listed above.

3. Use the paper trophies or other symbols as visible reminders of the deeds. If using paper trophies, glue or tape the trophies to the flip chart paper.

Key Questions

- How does it feel to think about what the team does right?
- Why is thinking about what the team does right important?
- Which flip chart has the most items?
- Why is it important to get results on both charts?
- What can we do to increase the number of items on the chart with the lower amount?

- How can we support one another so that we can achieve even more trophies?

A Word of Caution

A low-performing team on production, quality, or costs is still a low performing team no matter how well they interact. Therefore, the facilitator must always stress the need for results, as well as positive interaction. If a team has low production or low quality, the members will sometimes pass the blame onto others—the other department, another shift, market conditions, and so on. As the facilitator, you have to balance the discussion and be sure to get the team members to focus on themselves and the things that are within their control.

Variation

- If you have access to daily or weekly production, quality, or cost records that relate to your team's performance, make those records visible on charts or tables so everyone can see the results on a regular basis. You can also post accomplishments on the flip charts as milestones are reached. Then, once a month or at some other interval, you can pull the team together and discuss the progress.
- You can keep the flip charts as documents where team members can write accomplishments at any time. This would keep the team members thinking about positive accomplishments all the time, not just at their regular meeting time.

Ask for Commitment

At the end of the meeting, ask, "How might you be willing to use what we discussed today in your daily work?"

EQ 11 Thank You for the Gifts

Level of Risk

Medium

Purpose

The purpose of this activity is to help team members identify and acknowledge specific skills or gifts that their teammates bring to the team.

Why Is This Important?

Sometimes people are unaware of the skills they possess. When team members acknowledge each other's skills, it is a powerful attribution that serves to build positive team relations. Also, when team members acknowledge skills, they can sometimes make better use of a team member's natural gifts.

When to Use This Activity

This activity could be used anytime with a team. It is particularly useful if team members lose sight of the contributions and gifts that each member brings. It's also quite useful as a party or holiday event.

Set the Stage

State the obvious to the group—that everyone has different skills and abilities and that when we value and appreciate people's strengths, it's good for the team. In fact, discuss the idea that if everyone had the exact same skills, the team would suffer. You can use an example to make your point, such as if everyone on the football team were great at blocking but no one could catch the ball or run with it, the team would not be able to win a game.

Materials

Gift bags with each team member's name.

Gift cards—3 × 3 pieces of paper or cardstock with a picture of a gift on the front (Cards can be any size; 3 × 3 is just a suggestion.) See Handout 5-2 as an example.

The Activity

1. Give each team member one 3 × 3 gift card. (If there are 10 team members, each person should receive 10 blank gift cards.) Also each team member should receive a gift bag with his or her name on it.
2. On the front of each gift card, instruct the team members to write the name of each team member. Now, ask the team members to write on the back of the card a skill that person brings to the team. Instruct the team members to begin with, "Thanks for your . . ." Examples could be: Thanks for your organization skills. Thanks for your ability to help us see the big picture. Thanks for your ability to put customers at ease. Thanks for the fact that you always know how to fix the paper jams.
3. Instruct team members to place the finished gift card in the gift bag corresponding to the person's name.
4. Allow team members time to read their gift cards.

Key Questions

- Were you surprised by any of the cards you received?
- How do others' opinions of your gifts compare to your own?
- How does it feel to receive these gifts?
- How can you use your gifts to advance the team?
- Are people always aware of their gifts?
- What can you do to help others recognize their gifts?
- Once we are aware of our gifts, how can we use them to help others?
- How can our gifts be exploited?
- What can we do to be sure that we don't exploit the gifts of others?

A Word of Caution

Make sure everyone is instructed to do a gift card for all team members. Don't make it optional to do a gift card for only some members. If you do, it is possible that someone on the team will not receive any items and the exercise could backfire by creating negative feelings rather than positive feelings.

Variation

You can ask people to sign the gift cards or leave them anonymous. Signing the cards is preferred, but some groups may prefer anonymity.

Ask for Commitment

At the end of the meeting, ask, "What are you willing to do to let your teammates know about their gifts on a daily basis?"

HANDOUT 5-2 Example of a Gift Card

EQ 12 Who Said That?

Level of Risk

Medium

Purpose

The purpose of this exercise is to become aware of the effects certain repetitive thoughts can have on our performance or mindset. These thoughts, called voices, are repetitive in nature and tend to be ever present in our thinking. They can influence the way we behave. Sometimes the influence can be positive; other times, these thoughts can have a negative influence. As we become aware of these thoughts, we can choose to pay attention to them or to replace them with other thoughts that have a more desirable effect on our performance or behavior.

Why Is This Important?

Consciously choosing our behavior is important. When we consciously choose, we empower ourselves and set the standard for our own behavior. Otherwise, we behave at the will of others or as victims of our circumstances. However, sometimes our behavior is held hostage by our thinking patterns. It's important to recognize these thinking patterns and free ourselves to behave in a manner that is consistent with our intentions.

When to Use This Activity

This activity helps team members get to know one another on a deeper level. It is also useful if members are not living up to their potential because of repetitive thought patterns that might be holding them back.

Set the Stage

Talk to the group about different thinking patterns or "voices." Give some personal examples. Let the group know that, over time, thinking patterns can become ingrained and thereby influence behavior in ways that may be unknown to the individual. For example, if you tend to doubt yourself, the self-doubt could erode your confidence and, over time, you may behave in a more tentative way. You may doubt your ability to do certain tasks, make certain decisions, or state your opinions.

Materials

Refer to the Voices worksheet at the end of this chapter (see Handout 5-3).

The Activity

1. Hand out a copy of the Voices worksheet (Handout 5-3) to each participant.
2. Ask participants to think about the three or four voices that are most often present in their thought patterns. Ask group members to put a check next to the voices that are most prevalent in their thinking.
3. Ask group members to disclose these to the group.
4. Ask the group to comment on the selections.
5. Then ask group members to consider how these voices can interfere with their daily interactions and performance.

Key Questions

- ➤ How easy was it for you to recognize some of your voices?
- ➤ Was anyone surprised by the voices selected by their teammates?
- ➤ How can being aware of these voices or thought patterns be useful to you?
- ➤ How can being aware of these voices help your team?
- ➤ What can you do to overcome the thought patterns or voices that you have?
- ➤ Give some examples of things that you do to overcome negative thought patterns or voices.

- ➤ As a team, why is it useful to understand your team's patterns?
- ➤ How can teammates help one another to overcome these voices?

A Word of Caution

Just a note that it's probably useful to distinguish the voices or thought patterns that we are referring to in this exercise from psychotic voices. Psychotic voices are a symptom of a serious psychological impairment that requires medical attention. The voices that we speak of are simple themes in our thinking and are common for all people to experience. We use the word voice just to give character to the thought pattern, so it is easy to recognize.

Variation

Just as individuals have voices, teams also develop voices or patterns of thought. It is useful for the team to step back and assess the "voice" or thought pattern of the group. Is the group suffering from self-doubt? Does the group play victim—very often thinking that things are outside of its control? Does the group suffer from famine voice—very often concerned that there is not enough time, resources, or money to do the things it wants? Ask the team to determine if there is a particular voice or thought pattern that comes through and what the team can do to break this thought pattern.

Ask for Commitment

At the end of the meeting, ask, "How might you be willing to use what we discussed today in your daily work?"

HANDOUT 5-3 Voices: A Few Examples

NEGATIVE VOICES	POSITIVE VOICES
The Victim Voice says nothing is ever your fault; you are always a victim & you don't need to take responsibility for your life.	**The Good Seeker Voice** says there is good in everything and will find this goodness, even in difficult situations.
The Failure Voice tells you that you are a failure at everything you try and focuses on the past.	**The Abundance Voice** tells you that life's riches are plentiful, and believes that there will somehow always be enough.
The Voice of Revenge constantly mutters "just wait," and is biding time until ready to pounce.	**The Hope Voice** assures you that tomorrow will be bright, and has positive expectations about the future.
The Self-Doubt Voice constantly plants seeds of doubt in your mind, destroying confidence and killing your tomorrow.	**The Humor Voice** reminds you not to take life too seriously, finds what is silly or fun in everything, and encourages you to laugh.
The Egregious Injustice Voice is always telling you you've been wronged and dwells on injustice in every aspect of your life.	**The Gratitude Voice** always looks at the bright side of things, expressing thanks for everything, even in difficult situations.
The Famine Voice tells you there will never be enough of anything, causing you to constantly panic over resources.	**The Creative Voice** is all about imagination and innovation, and always finds new ways to approach life.
The "Ain't it Awful" Voice tells you that your fate is always awful, and makes a catastrophe out of everything.	**The Forgiveness Voice** encourages you to let go of grudges and anger, and accept others, reminding you that no one is perfect.

(continued)

HANDOUT 5-3 ***Continued***

NEGATIVE VOICES	POSITIVE VOICES
The Hide Voice always tells you to lie low and not take action.	**The What Role Did I Play Voice** asks you to look at situations to determine how you may have contributed to a negative event, not in order to assign blame, but to help you improve in the future.
The Pleaser Voice tries to get you to please everyone, and imposes guilt if you don't.	**The Faith Voice** assures you that whatever life holds, you'll be okay, and draws on a spiritual knowledge that permeates all aspects of life.
The Comparison Voice compares everything in your life with what others have, and lets you know how you rank.	**The Perspective Voice** reminds you of the facts and helps you get a grip on reality.
The Fix-It Voice claims it's your responsibility to fix everything in your life and in others' lives.	**The Honor Voice** encourages you to admire others and demonstrate your respect.
The Perfectionist Voice wants you and everything you do to be absolutely perfect, and will let you know when you fall short.	**The Optimist Voice** reminds you that things will turn out well.

EQ 13 Choir Director

Level of Risk

Medium

Purpose

Use this exercise to introduce the idea that people have the power to choose the thought patterns or voices that they wish to use to influence their behavior. It will also show team members how thoughts precede behavior. This exercise also gives team members an easy metaphor to remember for changing thoughts.

Why Is This Important?

It is very empowering to know that individuals have choices in their behavior and that those choices can be influenced by what the individual chooses to think about. In this exercise, team members will learn that they can control the influences over their behavior simply by changing their thoughts or voices. Individual team members are able to see that they can easily influence the climate of the team.

When to Use This Activity

This activity is useful at any time with a team. However, it should be used after the team has been exposed to the exercise "Who Said That?" because the team should be familiar with the concept of voices. It is particularly useful if the group doesn't seem to recognize their potential for controlling the climate of the team.

Set the Stage

Ask the group if they have ever observed a choir director directing the voices in a singing group. Ask the group to recall how the choir director sometimes asks for some members of the choir to sing louder, while directing other voices to sing softer. Depending on the desired effect, the director controls the volume and asks for the perfect combination of the voices to make wonderful music. Relate the analogy of the choir director to the different thoughts or voices in our heads competing for center stage in the choir. Someone must direct the thoughts, and that someone is our internal choir director.

Materials

A conducting baton is a useful prop for this exercise.
Copies of the Voices worksheet used in the exercise "Who Said That?" for each team member.

The Activity

1. Give the Voices worksheet (Handout 5-3) to the team members. Assign or ask for volunteers to play different voices on the worksheet. Be sure that approximately half the members are going to play negative voices and the other half positive voices.
2. Assign the group a task to think about. The task could be a real work task, such as redesigning the storeroom. Give the group members some time to think about how the "voice" they are assigned would sound when discussing the task. For example, the critic voice might say, "That will never work." Or, "The storeroom doesn't need to be redesigned; it just needs people to put things away." The blame voice might say, "It's not our fault the storeroom needs to be reorganized. We didn't mess it up. Why don't you have the maintenance people reorganize it?" Positive voices might be the optimist voice saying, "I'm sure we can come up with something." Other positive voices might include the abundance voice, "I'm sure we'll have time to reorganize it." Or the gratitude voice might say, "This is great. I appreciate the fact that we can arrange it the way that meets our needs. Let's get to work."
3. Give the team members some time to think about several phrases that might come to mind as they play the particular roles they are assigned.
4. The facilitator should begin the discussion about reorganizing the storeroom. He or she should instruct the team members with negative voices to speak and ask the team members with positive voices to remain silent.

5. Debrief by asking members to comment on the atmosphere of the discussion. Also, ask the team if the task is likely to get done with this type of "voice."

6. The facilitator should begin the discussion again about reorganizing the storeroom. This time, he or she should ask that only the positive voices speak and the negative voices remain silent.

7. Debrief by asking members to comment on the atmosphere of the discussion.

Key Questions

- How do the voices or thoughts in our head compete for the floor?
- How can you act as a choir director for these thoughts in your own head?
- What is the value of acting as a choir director for your thoughts?
- What is the difference between a thought and a remark that points out something negative versus a critical voice? (Remarks that point out negative consequences are important to the decision-making and problem solving process and are encouraged. A negative or critical voice is a constant pattern in our thinking that looks at everything in an effort to find something wrong. People who are always coming from the critical voice rarely express anything positive about a situation or change. Criticism is their mindset.)

A Word of Caution

If you pick an extremely controversial workplace topic, the learning from the exercise could be overpowered by the topic. Select a topic that will produce a relatively neutral reaction from the team.

Variation

Rather than a workplace issue, the facilitator could select general topics. Topics such as: Creating a playground for children in the vacant lot next door; Planning a party menu; Deciding on a vacation spot, and so on.

Ask for Commitment

At the end of the meeting, ask, "How might you be willing to use what we discussed today in your daily work?"

EQ 14 Five Team Strengths—A 360 Assessment

Level of Risk

Low

Purpose

The purpose of this exercise is for the team to recognize its greatest strengths and to discuss how these strengths can be leveraged for the good of the organization.

Why Is This Important?

It is important for the team to identify its greatest strengths. When a team understands its assets or strengths, it can use the strengths to solve problems and interact. The team will also be able to predict what types of assignments will be easiest because the assignment will play to the team's strengths.

When to Use This Activity

This activity is best used after the team has been functioning for long enough to have encountered both successes and challenges. If this exercise is used before a team has established a track record, the team will not have quality data and examples to discuss.

Set the Stage

Explain to the team that just as individuals have strengths and weaknesses, so do teams. Explain that when the team understands its strengths, it has the advantage of being able to leverage its strength.

Materials

Five Key Strengths worksheet to collect data from others (see Handout 5-4).

The Activity

1. Team members should identify five to ten people, including the team's manager or leader, as well as peers or other departments that the team interacts with on a regular basis. Team members can also use customers if they think it is appropriate. Ask team members to select people whom they think will give them honest feedback.

2. Team members should ask the people identified to think about their team and to list five words that describe the team's greatest strengths. Be sure people understand that you are not asking about individuals on the team, but rather the team as a whole. (You can assign this to various team members, so the entire process should take very little time.)

3. Team members should write the words they collected from the five to ten people on the worksheet.

4. Each team member should also participate in this exercise by writing five words that he or she thinks represent the team's five greatest strengths. Instruct the team to think about how the team functions on a daily basis and draw conclusions based on what the team does well.

5. Capture the team's answers on a second worksheet.

6. Ask team members to compare the team's answers by assessing the following:

    a. How is each team member's view of the team similar to each other's view?
    b. How is each team member's view of the team different from each other's view?
    c. How are the team members' views different from the outsiders' views of the team?
    d. How are the team members' views the same as the outsiders' views of the team?

Key Questions

- Why is getting opinions about strengths valuable?
- What surprised you?

- ➤ What were you able to predict?
- ➤ When can you use this information?
- ➤ What can you do to leverage strengths?

A Word of Caution

Be sure the team picks a fair sample of people to participate in the assessment. Also, be sure that the team understands that the purpose of getting outside feedback is to gain a true assessment of strengths.

Ask for Commitment

At the end of the meeting, ask, "How might you be willing to use what we discussed today in your daily work?"

HANDOUT 5-4 Five Key Strengths

NAME/DEPARTMENT	TEAM STRENGTHS				

EQ 15 Five Team Weaknesses—A 360 Assessment

Level of Risk

High

Purpose

The purpose of this exercise is for the team to recognize its greatest weaknesses, and to discuss how these weaknesses affect the organization and what can be done to overcome them.

Why Is This Important?

It is important for the team to understand its greatest weaknesses. When a team understands its weaknesses, it can devise strategies to overcome or compensate for them. The team will also be able to predict what types of assignments will present the greatest challenges because the assignment identifies the team's weaknesses.

When to Use This Activity

It is best to use this activity after the team has been functioning long enough to have encountered both successes and challenges. If this exercise is used before a team has established a track record, the team will not have good data to discuss.

Set the Stage

Explain to the team that just as individuals have strengths and weaknesses, so do teams. Explain that when the team understands its weaknesses, it has the advantage of being able to compensate for the weaknesses in some way.

Materials

Five Key Weaknesses worksheet to collect data from others (see Handout 5-5).

The Activity

1. Team members should identify five to ten people, including the team's manager or leader, as well as peers or other departments that the team interacts with on a regular basis. Team members can also use customers if they think it is appropriate. Ask team members to select people whom they think will give them honest feedback.
2. Team members should ask the people identified to think about their team and to list five words that speak to the team's greatest weakness. Be sure people understand that you are not asking about individuals on the team, but rather the team as a whole. (You can assign this to various team members, so the entire process should take very little time.)
3. Team members should write the words they collected from the five to ten people on the worksheet.
4. Each team member should also participate in this exercise by writing five words that he or she thinks represent the team's five greatest weaknesses. Instruct the team to think about how the team functions on a daily basis and draw conclusions based on what the team demonstrates as a weakness.
5. Capture the team's answers on a second worksheet.
6. Ask team members to compare the team's answers by assessing the following:
    - **a.** How is each team member's view of the team similar to each other's view?
    - **b.** How is each team member's view of the team different from each other's view?
    - **c.** How are the team members' views different from the outsiders' views of the team?
    - **d.** How are the team members' views the same as the outsiders' views of the team?

Key Questions

- ➤ Why is getting opinions about weaknesses valuable?
- ➤ What surprised you?
- ➤ What were you able to predict?
- ➤ When can you use this information?
- ➤ What can you do to address the weaknesses?

A Word of Caution

Just be sure that the team picks a fair sample of people to participate in the assessment. Also, be sure that the team understands that the purpose of getting outside feedback is to gain a true assessment of weaknesses. In the event that the team is performing very poorly with customers, use caution when asking customers their opinions. Unless the team is prepared to follow through with some intense action planning, asking customers their opinions and then doing nothing with the information may cause more harm than good.

Variation

At the end of each team meeting or at some other regular interval, you can ask the group to comment on how well the group used its strengths and overcame its weaknesses. This can keep the idea of strengths and weaknesses visible to the team.

Ask for Commitment

At the end of the meeting, ask, "How might you be willing to use what we discussed today in your daily work?"

HANDOUT 5-5 Five Key Weaknesses

NAME/DEPARTMENT	TEAM WEAKNESSES				

This handout is available in pdf form at http://www.amacombooks.org/quickElact

EQ 16 Speak Up

Level of Risk

Medium

Purpose

The purpose of this exercise is to encourage people to speak up in team meetings about issues that are important to them. Sometimes people are reluctant to speak up for a variety of reasons. This exercise encourages people to speak up, and it sets the tone for team meetings as a place to speak up and be heard.

Why Is This Important?

If people do not speak up, issues can sometimes go underground and fester. Team members can also look for support outside the team meetings, thus creating a divide or gulf within the team because team members are asked to choose sides. Also, team members can learn that speaking up and expressing ideas are good for the team, even if those ideas are not popular.

When to Use This Activity

This is a good exercise to use when the group is still forming norms and establishing ground rules for successful meetings. It is also useful to use this exercise if some members tend to dominate meetings and others are routinely quiet.

Set the Stage

Ask the group if anyone has ever had the experience of walking away from a meeting wishing they had said something, or feeling that their voice wasn't heard. Sometimes we don't speak up because we're not confident about our idea or comment. At other times, we feel as though the more dominant members would only drown our idea or comment out. Still other times, perhaps meeting times run short or the group is just in a rush to get through the agenda, so the ideas or comments of some are just left unsaid.

Materials

A microphone, talking stick, or some other physical symbol that serves as a visible reminder of who has the floor during a meeting.

The Activity

1. The facilitator introduces the microphone or the talking stick and says that during the team meeting, team members must have physical possession of the microphone or talking stick in order to address the group.
2. Also, the facilitator will pass the microphone or talking stick to teammates who have not spoken up and ask them to please state their ideas or opinions about the subject the team is discussing.
3. The facilitator should encourage the group to get in the habit of using this device at future meetings so the group gets in the habit of sharing the floor with all members of the team.

Key Questions

- What is the advantage of using a talking stick or microphone to signify the speaker?
- During our past meetings, which of our teammates tended to have the talking stick more often?
- Which team members do we hear the least from?
- What are some of the reasons some people speak up and others remain silent?
- What is the best way to present an idea that is contrary to the team's direction? Give some ideas about how to present such an idea?
- Why is it important for contrary ideas or opinions to be heard?
- What is the difference between a contrary idea and "nay-saying"?
- As a fellow team member, what can you do to encourage everyone's ideas?

A Word of Caution

If one member of the group clearly dominates the discussion, it's probably a good idea to thank the person who dominates by acknowledging your appreciation of his or her willingness to share his or her opinions and then to state that the intention of this exercise isn't to silence this person, but rather to ensure that other members' voices are heard equally.

Ask for Commitment

At the end of the meeting, ask, "How might you be willing to use what we discussed today in your daily work?"

EQ 17 Keep Your Eye on the Eye

Level of Risk

High

Purpose

The purpose of this exercise is to help group members recognize that eye contact is an important nonverbal communication tool. Eye contact during group discussions can communicate different things to team members, who should pay particular attention to eye contact during conversations to improve communications.

Why Is This Important?

More than 70 percent of what we communicate is nonverbal. Eye contact is especially important because of the amount of data that is communicated through the eyes. When speaking to one another, eye contact can communicate respect for the other person. Eye contact can denote acknowledgement; it can say, "You matter," or "I hear your point of view," or "I respect you enough to give you the floor." Depending on the situation, eye contact can also say, "I disapprove of you or your opinion." In this way, eye contact can be a challenge. In either case the person receiving the eye contact is visible. Lack of eye contact can make people feel invisible, as if their point of view is unimportant.

When to Use This Activity

This powerful exercise can be used at many different times. It can be used when the team is still in its early stage and patterns of interaction have not yet been established. It can also be used to draw attention to and disrupt an established power hierarchy. Always use this exercise with caution. It can be very threatening to receive this type of feedback.

Set the Stage

Tell the team members that you will be videotaping a meeting so that you can examine the nonverbal interactions of the team. Explain that nonverbal interactions are extremely difficult to be aware of and that this exercise will help the members gain awareness of their nonverbal communications during team meetings. Do not tell the group that the specific nonverbal cue you will be focusing on is eye contact.

Materials

Ideally, the facilitator should have two video cameras set up so that they capture the faces of all participants.

Video playback device

The Activity

1. The facilitator should do this exercise when something important is on the agenda. It should be something that the team members definitely have opinions about or have a vested interest in. In fact, any item about which teammates have a strong difference of opinion is a good discussion to videotape.
2. Instruct team members to just forget about the camera and discuss the agenda item as usual. Once the team has entered into the discussion, roll the videotapes.
3. The facilitator can play back the entire tapes or select the portions that would be most useful for discussion.

Key Questions

- What did you observe about the eye contact of each individual on the team?
- Who made eye contact with whom?
- What do you think the eye contact signified?
- How did it feel if you did not receive any eye contact from the speaker? (Depending on the issue, it could feel good or bad. If the speaker was not making eye contact because he or she did not acknowledge the person's position or opinion, the person on the

receiving end could feel invisible. On the other hand, if the speaker was making eye contact with someone to challenge or prove a point, the person could feel challenged or threatened. So the eye contact must be put in the context of the conversation.)

- Have you ever been in a situation where someone did not make eye contact with you when you were making a point? How did it make you feel? What impact could that have on teamwork?
- Have you ever been in a situation where someone made eye contact with you in a manner that seemed challenging? How did it make you feel? What impact could that have on teamwork?
- After watching the tape, what changes would you wish to make to the level of eye contact and manner of interaction?

A Word of Caution

Depending on the team's comfort level with one another, this could be a very threatening discussion. However, the level of learning from this exercise can be very high. You'll have to assess whether your team is able to handle the honesty that this exercise could produce. Videotape doesn't lie! This exercise takes more time than most of the other exercises in this book; however, the results could be well worth the effort.

Variation

Another variation of this exercise is to tape the meeting, but to invite the persons in the meeting to view the tape privately. During this private viewing, you can debrief with the same type of questions. This variation is much less threatening than conducting the debrief period in front of the entire team.

Once you have the tape, there are several other items that the team members could work on, such as how they present their ideas, how they react to what others say, and other nonverbal communication or body language besides eye contact.

Ask for Commitment

After the meeting, ask, "How might you be willing to use what we discussed today in your daily work?"

EQ 18 My Dirty Dozen

Level of Risk

High

Purpose

The purpose of this exercise is for team members to help one another identify thought processes or beliefs called the "Dirty Dozen." The Dirty Dozen are common thought patterns or beliefs that interfere with our rational thinking and cause reactions that are inappropriate or out of proportion to the actual event. For example, one of the Dirty Dozen is a belief that you must be perfect at all times and cannot make a mistake. Of course, this belief is irrational because as humans we are prone to error. However, if we suffer from this irrational belief, our reaction to being caught making even a slight mistake could be very exaggerated. We could feel embarrassed, ashamed, get angry, feel humiliated or some other reaction that is just inappropriate for the circumstance.

Why Is This Important?

It's important for team members to be aware of the Dirty Dozen because when the Dirty Dozen are present in our thinking, we can have reactions that are not conducive to teamwork. Just imagine what reaction you might get confronting a teammate about a routine error if that teammate feels that he or she cannot make a mistake. Rather than being inquisitive about the error and learning more about it, the teammate may feel humiliated and react inappropriately. So, as people become increasingly aware of beliefs that can interfere with the smooth functioning of the team, all members of the team will benefit.

When to Use This Activity

Anytime. This exercise is very useful to help team members gain self-awareness. It also can be fun if done in a lighthearted manner.

Set the Stage

Explain to the group that there are 12 commonly held beliefs called the "Dirty Dozen" that are irrational and that can impair a person's functioning on a team or in life. It's important to discuss these commonly held beliefs, so that people can understand them and learn which ones affect them.

Materials

A list of the Dirty Dozen (see Handout 5-6).

The Activity

1. Give each person a copy of the Dirty Dozen.
2. Discuss and give examples of the Dirty Dozen.
3. Be sure to tell the group that all of us suffer from thinking or beliefs that are irrational, which we are calling the Dirty Dozen. Explain that depending on the person, some are more common to our thinking than others.
4. Ask the group members to study the list and determine which ones are most common in their thinking.
5. Ask each group member to tell the group the one or two items that are common to him or her and, if possible, give an example.

Key Questions

- ➤ Why is it important to be aware of the Dirty Dozen that affect our thinking?
- ➤ Once aware of the Dirty Dozen, how can we use this information?
- ➤ Looking at each of the Dirty Dozen, what impact can each have on a team?
- ➤ What are some things we can do to mitigate the Dirty Dozen?
- ➤ How can releasing ourselves of the Dirty Dozen improve our ability to work together?

A Word of Caution

Some people may argue that the Dirty Dozen are positive and desirable. For example, it could be argued that not wanting to make a mistake or wishing to please others are positive qualities. Although that's true, help the team to understand that when a person always has to please others or is never comfortable making a mistake, that's unreasonable and can interfere with his or her functioning. Remember, we're not trying to disregard pleasing others or being error free, we're just trying to determine how our thinking can interfere with our functioning.

Variation

It is much easier to see this in other people. We are often blind to our own "Dirty Dozen." If the trust level of the group is high, it would be very useful to ask the group to comment when the person states his or her Dirty Dozen. This increases the risk level of the activity, but it also increases the insight that people gain.

Ask for Commitment

After the meeting, ask, "How might you be willing to use what we discussed today in your daily work?"

HANDOUT 5-6 The Dirty Dozen

1. **Needing Approval:** "Everyone I work with must approve of me at all times."
2. **Making Mistakes:** "I must prove thoroughly competent, adequate, and achieving at all times."
3. **Changing Others:** "I have an obligation to change others who act unfairly or obnoxiously."
4. **Catastrophize:** "When I get very frustrated, treated unfairly or rejected, I have to view things as awful, terrible, horrible and catastrophic."
5. **Others Cause Misery:** "My emotional misery comes from external pressures that I have little ability to change."
6. **Worry, Fret, and Fear:** "If something seems dangerous or fearsome, I must preoccupy myself with it and make myself anxious about it."
7. **Avoidance:** "It's easier to avoid facing difficulties and self-responsibilities than to do something about them."
8. **The Past:** "My past remains all–important, and because something once strongly influenced my life, it has to keep determining my feelings and behavior today."
9. **Unrealistic Expectations:** "People and things should turn out better than they do, and I must fix them."
10. **Competition:** "My worth can be measured by competitive situations."
11. **Source of Problems:** "The people and conditions in my life are the source of my problems."
12. **Negativity:** "Certain occurrences or events are negative by nature."

EQ 19 Search Warrants for the Dirty Dozen

Level of Risk

High

Purpose

The purpose of this activity is to help team members gain awareness "in the moment" of thought processes that may be contributing to unwanted behavior. To become aware "in the moment" is a very valuable gift, because it gives us the luxury of thinking about alternative ways to proceed in our interactions with others.

Why Is This Important?

When we are able to confront our thinking, we are then empowered to change it. Without being aware of our thought patterns, we will continue to act or react in the same way. By challenging the way we think about things, we may be able to determine if there is a more productive way to behave. True power comes from being able to choose how we wish to behave and being aware "in the moment" of the thought patterns that could sabotage those efforts. The Dirty Dozen are common, irrational thinking patterns that sabotage our behavior.

Set the Stage

Open with the following question, "Wouldn't it be great if someone could follow you around and catch you before you do something you regret?" Ask the group to imagine how useful it would be if a little buzzer could go off to warn you that your thinking is about to get you into trouble. Explain that this activity is designed to help team members help each other.

When to Use This Activity

This exercise can be fun and lighthearted, especially when the team gets along well. It is a great way to gain increased self-awareness through the feedback of others.

Materials

Mock search warrants (see Handout 5-7).
A list of the Dirty Dozen visible on the wall or flip chart (see Handout 5-6).

The Activity

1. Keep a stack of search warrants in your meeting or work area.
2. Ask the team members to present search warrants to fellow teammates when they suspect the teammate may be harboring one of the Dirty Dozen based on a comment or reaction that the teammate displays.
3. Encourage teammates to issue warrants right at the moment when they hear the Dirty Dozen.

Key Questions

- How is getting caught in the act important to furthering our self-awareness?
- How can being aware of the Dirty Dozen in our thinking improve our quality of life and work?

A Word of Caution

Although this is a very serious activity in terms of what a person can learn, be sure to keep the activity lighthearted. Being singled out can cause someone to become defensive. You may need to coach people to realize that feedback "in the moment" is a gift, and the best response when someone gives you a gift is to say thank you. If your team members don't respect one another, this activity probably isn't the best choice. Work to build trust first; then introduce this activity at a later time.

Variation

Create your team's own version of the Dirty Dozen. Help the team identify some critical mistakes in thinking that impact teamwork. Use those as the basis of this exercise.

Ask for Commitment

After the meeting, ask, "How might you be willing to use what we discussed today in your daily work?"

HANDOUT 5-7 Search Warrant

We have searched and found the following irrational items in your thinking:

Name of Suspect: ________________ Name of Officer: ______________

Place a check (✓) next to all that apply.

- ☐ **Needing Approval:** "Everyone I work with must approve of me at all times."
- ☐ **Making Mistakes:** "I must prove thoroughly competent, adequate, and achieving at all times."
- ☐ **Changing Others:** "I have an obligation to change others who act unfairly or obnoxiously."
- ☐ **Catastrophize:** "When I get very frustrated, treated unfairly, or rejected, I have to view things as awful, terrible, horrible and catastrophic."
- ☐ **Others Cause Misery:** "My emotional misery comes from external pressures that I have little ability to change."
- ☐ **Worry, Fret, and Fear:** "If something seems dangerous or fearsome, I must preoccupy myself with it and make myself anxious about it."
- ☐ **Avoidance:** "It's easier to avoid facing difficulties and self-responsibilities than to do something about them."
- ☐ **The Past:** "My past remains all–important, and because something once strongly influenced my life, it has to keep determining my feelings and behavior today."
- ☐ **Unrealistic Expectations:** "People and things should turn out better than they do, and I must fix them."
- ☐ **Competition:** "My worth can be measured by competitive situations."
- ☐ **Source of Problems:** "The people and conditions in my life are the source of my problems."
- ☐ **Negativity:** "Certain occurrences or events are negative by nature."

EQ 20 PFAT Self-Scan

Level of Risk

High

Purpose

The purpose of this exercise is to raise self-awareness, especially during high-stress or conflict situations. By using a four-point checklist, individuals can become aware of how they react under pressure.

Why Is This Important?

People are more prone to negative behaviors when they are experiencing conflict or high stress. During conflict or high stress situations, the body reacts with increased heart rate, dry mouth, and sweaty palms. Also, if we pay attention to our emotions during conflict or high stress situations, we typically feel anxious, defensive, worried, attacked, challenged, angry, scared, or threatened. When we're feeling this way, our thinking can become fixated on defending ourselves, discrediting others, or redeeming ourselves. Also, our body language often supports these positions and, therefore, we appear to others to be in a highly stressed state.

When to Use This Activity

Use this activity when the team has obvious issues surrounding a conflict. You can also use this exercise to teach people the self-scan technique, so the team members will be more aware of their reactions to high stress and conflict. Then, when a team conflict arises, ask the group to do the PFAT Self-Scan.

Set the Stage

Most people have difficulty managing conflict. The two most common reactions are fight or flight, but in an organizational setting, neither of these reactions is productive. Most conflict resolution requires that individuals discuss differences, determine mutual ground, find ways to mutually benefit each other, and solve differences in a way that maintains their relationship. However, often, individuals begin fight or flight behavior long before they are aware that they are in a conflict situation. For example, they avoid certain unpleasant situations or don't speak up during the early stages of a discussion or they defend themselves when someone is just asking a question to gain information. These negative behaviors can be the result of a brewing conflict, but the individual doesn't recognize the fight or flight nature of these encounters. After a while, the conflict can escalate. By employing a simple technique known as the PFAT scan, individuals can gain valuable information that can improve their self-awareness during conflict or high stress situations. The PFAT scan includes the following self-check:

1) What is my **Physical** body telling me? Heart rate? Dry mouth? Sweaty palms? Clenched teeth?

2) What am I **Feeling**? Anxious? Tense? Angry? Defensive? Attacked? Worried? Scared? Challenged?

3) How do I **Appear** to others? Lunging forward? Glaring? Avoiding? Yelling? Hesitant? Stammering? Sheepish?

4) On what is my **Thinking** focused? Defending my position? Discrediting others? Redeeming myself?

Materials

A handout prepared with the PFAT Self-Scan Checklist (see Handout 5-8).

Flip chart.

The Activity

1. List a controversial topic on the flip chart and divide the flip chart sheet in half. On one side, write Pro and on the other side write Con.

2. Ask group members to select a side based on their true opinions about the topic.

3. Set the chairs or tables facing one another.

4. Ask the group to debate the issue and defend their Pro or Con position.

5. Once the discussion heats up, stop the discussion and ask people to do a PFAT Self-Scan check.
6. Ask members to discuss what they discovered during the PFAT Self-Scan.
7. Ask the opposing group members to give feedback regarding anything they observed related to PFAT in their opponents.

Key Questions

- How do you think your behavior changed from the beginning stages of the discussion to the end stages of the discussion?
- What impact do you think your reaction may have had on others?
- How can being aware through a PFAT Scan help us in our interactions?
- Do you think our behavior could be different if we are aware earlier in the conflict?
- How could being aware of our behavior earlier in a conflict help us and our team's interactions?

A Word of Caution

It will be difficult for people to stop the discussion and talk about what they are experiencing. However, you should coach them to focus on the PFAT Scan and let the topic rest.

Variation

Be sure you select topics about which people have strong opinions. You may have to repeat the discussion using two or three different topics to ensure that each person has a strong reaction and can experience the power of the PFAT Scan. Topics can be related to the organization or can be general topics sure to cause a difference of opinion.

Before you give the team the information contained in the "Set the Stage" section, you can have the team engage in the activity. Then, you can introduce the idea of the PFAT and ask them if they could comment on what they observed in themselves and in those who disagreed with them.

Ask for Commitment

After the meeting, ask, "How might you be willing to use what we discussed today in your daily work?"

HANDOUT 5-8 PFAT Self-Scan Checklist	
Physical	Heart rate? Dry mouth? Sweaty palms? Clenched teeth?
Feeling	Anxious? Tense? Angry? Defensive? Attacked? Worried? Scared? Challenged?
Appearance	Lunging forward? Glaring? Avoiding? Yelling? Hesitant? Stammering? Sheepish?
Thinking	Defending my position? Discrediting others? Redeeming myself?

EQ 21 PFAT Group Scan

Level of Risk

High

Purpose

The purpose of this exercise is to help team members become more aware of the reactions of others on the team. By scanning the group using a four-point checklist, individuals can become more aware of how others are reacting in a group meeting.

Why Is This Important?

It's important for us to understand the reaction of others. As we heighten our awareness of these reactions, we can become more aware of our impact on them. In addition, we can choose to interact in a way that is less threatening or otherwise more productive for the outcomes we desire. Especially when under stress or in conflict, being aware of how people are reacting can give us valuable information that enables us to determine how or when to adjust our approach. As we learned in the PFAT Self-Scan, during conflict or in high stress situations, the body reacts with increased heart rate, dry mouth, and sweaty palms, and we typically feel anxious, defensive, worried, attacked, challenged, angry, scared, or threatened. As a result, our thinking can be distorted and our body language often reflects the stress.

When to Use This Activity

Use this activity when the team has obvious issues during a conflict. You can also use this exercise to teach people the scan technique, so that team members will be more aware of and sensitive to the reactions of their teammates.

Set the Stage

Most people have difficulty managing conflict. The two most common reactions are fight or flight, but in an organizational setting, neither of these reactions is productive. Most conflict resolution requires that individuals discuss differences, determine mutual ground, find ways to mutually benefit each other, and solve differences in a way that maintains their relationship. However, often, individuals begin fight or flight behavior long before they are aware that they are in a conflict situation. For example, they avoid certain unpleasant situations or don't speak up during the early stages of a discussion or they defend themselves when someone is just asking a question to gain information. These negative behaviors can be the result of a brewing conflict, but the individual doesn't recognize the fight or flight nature of these encounters. After a while, the conflict can escalate. By employing a simple technique known as the PFAT scan, individuals can gain valuable information that can improve their awareness during conflict or high stress situations. The PFAT scan can be applied to a group to include the following:

1) What **Physical** body symptoms do you observe in team members? Although you can't be aware of someone's heart rate or whether they have dry mouth, you may be able to observe other physical signs of stress: Sweaty palms? Clenched teeth? Nervous tics? Clenched fists? Sweating?

2) What might this person be **Feeling**? You are unable to know what another person is feeling, but you can draw some conclusions based on a person's behavior and then check those conclusions by active listening. Could the person be Anxious? Tense? Angry? Defensive? Attacked? Worried? Scared? Challenged?

3) What body language does the person **Appear** to have? Lunging forward? Glaring? Avoiding? Yelling? Hesitant? Stammering? Sheepish?

4) What is the person's **Thinking** focused on? Defending his or her position? Discrediting others? Redeeming him or her self?

Materials

A handout prepared with the PFAT Group-Scan Checklist (see Handout 5-9).

Flip chart.

The Activity

1. List a controversial topic on the flip chart and divide the flip chart in half. On one side, write Pro, and on the other side, write Con.
2. Ask group members to select a side based on their true opinions related to the topic.
3. Set the chairs or tables facing one another.
4. Ask the group to debate the issue and defend their Pro or Con position on the topic.
5. Once the discussion gets heated, stop the discussion and ask people to do a PFAT Group-Scan check.
6. Ask the opposite group to give feedback regarding anything they observed related to PFAT in those who disagreed with them.

Key Questions

- What did you learn about your behavior during conflict or high stress?
- What surprised you that your teammates were able to observe?
- What do you think your teammates missed about your behavior, thoughts, or feelings?
- What impact do you think your reaction may have had on others?
- How can you change your reaction during a conflict situation?
- Why is it useful to observe others in a conflict situation?
- How can being aware of others in a conflict situation change the outcome of the situation?
- How can empathy be improved when we practice a PFAT Group Scan?
- Why is improving empathy important?

A Word of Caution

It will be difficult for people to stop the discussion and talk about what they are experiencing. However, you should coach them to focus on the PFAT Scan and let the topic rest.

Variation

- The topics that you select should be topics about which people have a strong opinion. You may have to repeat the discussion using two or three different topics to ensure that each person has a strong reaction and can experience the power of the PFAT Scan. Topics can be related to the organization or can be general topics sure to cause a difference of opinion.
- Before you give the team the information contained in the "Set the Stage" section, you can have the team do the activity. Then, you can introduce the idea of the PFAT and ask them if they could comment on what they observed in themselves and their opponents.

Ask for Commitment

After the meeting, ask, "How might you be willing to use what we discussed today in your daily work?"

HANDOUT 5-9 PFAT Group-Scan Checklist

Physical What can you observe about the other people in the group?	Sweaty palms? Clenched teeth? Nervous tics? Clenched fists? Sweating? Turning red?
Feeling Since you can't observe someone's feelings, use active listening to verify your perceptions.	Anxious? Tense? Angry? Defensive? Attacked? Worried? Scared? Challenged?
Appearance	Lunging forward? Glaring? Avoiding? Yelling? Hesitant? Stammering? Sheepish?
Thinking	Defending their positions? Discrediting others? Redeeming themselves?

EQ 22 People and Perceptions

Level of Risk

Low

Purpose

The purpose of this activity is to increase self-awareness about how our preconceived ideas about people and events influence our interactions.

Why Is This Important?

All day long, people interact with one another in a team or work environment. We like to think of ourselves as open minded about those interactions, but we often have preconceived ideas about people or events. These preconceived ideas shape our reaction to the people and events before the event or encounter even occurs. Sometimes, our preconceived ideas bend our reaction in a positive way; at other times, it bends our reaction in a negative way. Rather than tout open mindedness, it may be more productive to understand and be aware of our preconceptions, so that we can caution ourselves not to prejudge.

When to Use This Activity

Anytime. By developing the skill of suspending judgment and preconceived ideas and opinions, you are teaching the team an essential EQ skill.

Set the Stage

It's best if this exercise has little explanation. If you tell people the premise and why it's important, it will be more difficult for people to acknowledge their preconceptions. So, begin the exercise by saying, "Let's have some fun today by taking a lighthearted look at celebrities and other people or places in the news."

Materials

Magazine pictures, newspaper headlines, videoclips or other items. It is useful to find pictures or images that are open to controversy.

A piece of paper for each participant, numbered 1–20.

The Activity

1. The facilitator should tell the group that he or she is going to hold up a photo, headline, or image.
2. Instruct the individuals in the group to jot down a few words of any random thoughts or first impressions they have about the photo, headline, or image. It's important to be relatively vague about the instructions, but stress the importance of first impressions.
3. Also, instruct the group to be sure to write something about how they feel or what they think about the image.
4. Repeat for at least 20 photos or headlines.
5. After teammates have completed writing down their first impressions, show each image again, and ask teammates to share any ideas they wrote down.

Key Questions

- ➤ Were your thoughts the same as your teammates'?
- ➤ What did you notice that was different? The same?
- ➤ What do you think influenced our thoughts?
- ➤ What impact can our preconceived thoughts have about a situation or encounter?
- ➤ In the workplace, do we have preconceived thoughts about people and encounters?
- ➤ What impact can these thoughts have on coworkers? Customers? Peers? Others?
- ➤ How can being aware of our preconceived thoughts about people, events, or encounters help us? Or hurt us?

A Word of Caution

This activity could point out obvious prejudices. If this occurs, it can be a powerful learning experience. It's important for the leader to be sensitive to the team members and determine if anyone's comments are offensive. If this occurs, the facilitator should use it as a learning experience regarding preconceived negative thoughts and their impact.

Variation

A much higher risk of this exercise would be to post pictures of teammates, peers, bosses, customers, or others, and ask for a quick opinion about the person or encounter. You can also do this with company or organizational initiatives—just throw out situations within the organization and quickly have people jot down their opinions or impression of the initiative or person. The debrief questions should be related to how opinions can affect our behavior related to these events or people.

Ask for Commitment

After the meeting, ask, "How might you be willing to use what we discussed today in your daily work?"

EQ 23 Tuning In

Level of Risk

Low

Purpose

The purpose of this exercise is to help team members tune in to their thoughts and internal dialogue. Sometimes, people are unaware of their internal dialogue and, therefore, they do not recognize the power that their internal dialogue has on their actions and behaviors.

Why Is This Important?

As people become aware of their internal thoughts and dialogue, they become more capable of managing their actions. True control of our behaviors requires an awareness of our internal thoughts and their influence on us, particularly because they can draw attention to preconceived thoughts we have about others and about events. Once we are aware, we can consciously decide how we wish to behave.

When to Use This Activity

Anytime. This exercise is a great way to increase self-awareness and can lead to greater teamwork, as team members realize how their internal dialogue can affect their behavior in the team.

Set the Stage

Explain to team members that the purpose of this exercise is to help them tune in to their internal dialogue. Define internal dialogue as the mental chatter, or private thoughts, that are present in our minds, but not spoken. (Many popular television shows or movies will run an audiotrack of the main characters where the viewer can hear their private thoughts. If the facilitator wishes, he or she could use one of these clips to help people understand the concept.) Explain to the team that if we analyze our private dialogue, we can gain much self-awareness.

Materials

A piece of paper for each team member.

The Activity

1. During a regular team meeting, give each team member a piece of paper and ask them to number it from 1–20.
2. At random points during the meeting, pause and ask the group members to tune in to their internal dialogue or private thoughts.
3. Ask group members to jot down their internal dialogue or private thoughts on the paper. (Ensure the team members that you won't ask them to share the content of their thoughts. After all, they are private thoughts.)

Key Questions

- Was it easy to tune in to your internal dialogue?
- Without sharing the actual thoughts, what trends or patterns did you see in your internal dialogue?
- As you look at your internal dialogue, what impact could it have had on your behavior or performance in the meeting?
- If you think about all the people and events you encounter during the course of the day, is your internal dialogue always active?
- Why is awareness of your internal dialogue important?
- Can internal dialogue be changed?
- If so, why might you want to change it?
- How would you change it?

A Word of Caution

Don't press people to share the content of their internal dialogue. The point of this exercise isn't to share the internal dialogue with others, but rather to increase awareness of the dialogue and how it could influence behavior.

Variation

Ask team members to perform this activity throughout the course of their workday. Instruct people to stop every half an hour and jot down their internal dialogue. Then, at the next team meeting, debrief the exercise.

Ask for Commitment

After the meeting, ask, "How might you be willing to use what we discussed today in your daily work?"

EQ 24 But I Didn't Mean . . .

Level of Risk

Medium

Purpose

The purpose of this exercise is to think about the result of our behavior rather than the intention of our behavior. By focusing on the results, we're better able to see the behavior from the other person's point of view. This improves our empathy and our ability to resolve conflict. This exercise helps participants examine their behavior, so they can determine what behavior could have been changed to achieve a better result.

Why Is This Important?

Not all, but many conflicts and misunderstandings result from a gap between our intentions and the end result of our behavior. Sometimes, we act in a way that is inconsistent with our intentions. Other times, we act in a way that we think is consistent with our intentions, but the person on the receiving end has a different perspective. The more skilled we are at aligning our intentions and our behavior, the more successful we will be in our relationships with others. When we act in a manner that is inconsistent with our intentions, it is very helpful to examine how and what we could have done to better align intentions and actions.

When to Use This Activity

This activity can be used at any time with your team. It is particularly useful if the team members have experienced a misunderstanding or conflict.

Set the Stage

Talk to the team about the word "intention." Ask the members to share their ideas about the meaning of the word intention. Explain that our intentions are not visible to the people with whom we interact. The only way that intention becomes visible is through behavior and words. Give some personal examples of when intention and behavior are aligned and misaligned.

Materials

Intentions Worksheet (see Handout 5-10).

The Activity

1. Give each team member a worksheet.
2. Ask the team members to think about an incident where their intentions didn't match their words or behaviors.
3. Ask them to complete the worksheet.

Key Questions

- ➤ What is the benefit of reflecting on occasions when our intention did not have the intended result?
- ➤ How can we use this information to improve our interactions with others?
- ➤ Why is it important to think about an alternative way to behave? (By thinking about an alternative way that we could have behaved, we are preparing ourselves and practicing so that we are better equipped for the next occasion.)
- ➤ What can we do after the fact? (Talking about the situation with the other party is always recommended so we can clear the air. It also gives you an opportunity to offer an apology and to fully understand the other person's perspective.)

A Word of Caution

If you use this exercise after a team misunderstanding or conflict, be especially careful to ensure that team members do not blame the other person by saying such things as, "You misunderstood," or "You're overly sensitive," or "You didn't listen to me." The purpose of this exercise is to help participants examine their behavior and how that behavior could have been changed to achieve a better result.

Ask for Commitment

After the meeting, ask, "How might you be willing to use what we discussed today in your daily work?"

HANDOUT 5-10 Intentions Worksheet

I SAID OR DID . . .	I MEANT . . .	THE RESULT . . .	I COULD HAVE SAID . . .
Example: "I didn't think it was a big deal."	I thought we could get it done without much effort.	You thought I didn't think it was important.	"I'd be happy to help. I don't think it will take very long to complete. When would you like to begin?"

EQ 25 Trading Spaces

Level of Risk

Low

Purpose

The purpose of this activity is to help team members gain a better understanding of one another. This exercise will require those teammates who are more talkative and assertive to trade places with teammates who are less talkative and assertive. In this exchange, team members will see the world from the other's point of view. It will improve the empathy of the group and will further develop the dynamics of the team.

Why Is This Important?

It's important for teammates to see the world from the other's viewpoint. Our natural tendency to be either talkative or quiet will be challenged. Through this challenge, we'll be able to experience the world from the other's viewpoint. Those who are more assertive will understand that those who are less assertive sometimes don't get an opportunity to speak. Those that are less assertive will understand that the more assertive participants are simply following long-established patterns of behavior. It's important for participants to recognize that the dynamics of the group will often shift when the balance of conversation shifts.

When to Use This Activity

This activity is particularly useful after the team has been functioning for some time, as it will help team members recognize the patterns and become sensitive to the other's perspective.

Set the Stage

Explain that some people by nature are more assertive than others. Explain that it's okay to be more assertive and it's okay to be less assertive.

The purpose of this exercise isn't to change anyone's natural tendency. Explain that when a group has been meeting for some time, patterns of dynamics form within the group. Once these patterns are formed, we don't really think much about the interactions of the team.

Materials

Tape.
A continuum drawn on a flip chart as such:

Lower Assertion	High Assertion
Asks questions	Tells opinions
Disagrees by asking	Disagrees by telling
Speaks less often	Speaks often
Thinks/processes inside	Thinks/processes out loud
Waits for others to speak	Speaks first
Defers to others' thoughts before stating own	States own thoughts first rather than wait for others
Thinks before speaking	Speaks then thinks

The Activity

1. Place tape on the floor to signify the continuum. Label one end High Assertion and the other end Lower Assertion. Mark the middle of the continuum.
2. Ask the team members to place themselves on the continuum as they see themselves within the team. Instruct the team members to stand anywhere except right in the middle.
3. Ask the team members now to place themselves on the continuum at one extreme or the other depending on where they stood relative to the middle. (Tell the team that you recognize that the extremes may not be an adequate description or fit. However, for the sake of this exercise you are asking that they determine which end better describes them.)
4. Facilitate a discussion about something important to the team. You can select any topic that you think the team will have interest in.
5. During the discussion, ask the team members to figuratively trade places on the continuum scale. For example, if a team member

placed himself or herself on the high assertion side of the scale, during the course of the discussion, they should behave as if they possess the characteristics of lower assertion. Instruct these persons to count to ten slowly each time they wish to speak. For those people who placed themselves on the lower end of the assertion continuum, ask them to behave as if they possess the characteristics of higher assertion. Instruct these people to just start talking and see what comes out. You can coach them to use the words . . . "In my opinion . . ." and then just go with whatever comes to mind without thinking through their thoughts or opinions.

Key Questions

- Was this easy or difficult?
- What can we learn from trading spaces?
- When might it be appropriate to sometimes trade spaces?
- How did trading spaces change the dynamics of the team?
- What do you think would be the benefit of trading spaces?

Variation

You can have a poster made up for your meeting area. When the more assertive participants seem to be dominating the discussion, you could hold up the poster and ask people to trade spaces for a while.

Ask for Commitment

After the meeting, ask, "How might you be willing to use what we discussed today in your daily work?"

EQ 26 What Else?

Level of Risk

Low

Purpose

The purpose of this exercise is to determine how the team dynamics change when the flow of the meeting is interrupted with intentional breaks. These intentional breaks allow the discussion to travel in a different or deeper direction that sometimes uncovers important information that the team would normally skip.

Why Is This Important?

Sometimes, what comes out after the discussion has ended or after the decision is made is the most important information. It's what we say in the hall after the meeting that may be significant and could improve the decision or discussion. Because we're often rushed to get through an agenda, these items can be missed. By asking a simple question, "What else about this topic or decision should we consider?" and asking it several times until the discussion is truly depleted, rich information can be gained.

When to Use This Activity

Use this exercise when the team seems to rush through the agenda or rush to decisions. This exercise is useful in uncovering resistance or doubt about ideas that people may be reluctant to state. Also, people often don't want to bog down the team, so in an effort to appear to be a team player, they just move on to the next item. If you notice that team members often express ideas or opinions outside the team meeting about items discussed in the meeting, it may be a signal that this activity would be worthwhile. (It could also be a signal that you may need to have a ground rule about expressing ideas or opinions to the team versus outside the team.)

Set the Stage

There is no need for the facilitator to set the stage for this exercise. The facilitator should simply use the question frequently until the team has fully exhausted the discussion.

Materials

Flip chart and marker.

The Activity

During the regular team meeting, the facilitator should pause and ask the question, "What else about this topic or decision should we consider?" The facilitator should ask this question more than once before moving on to the next agenda item.

Key Questions

- At the end of the meeting, the facilitator can ask, "Have you noticed anything different about today's meeting?"
- In what ways was today's meeting better than other meetings?
- In what ways was today's meeting not as good as other meetings?

A Word of Caution

Don't use this exercise on a team that tends to over analyze things or discuss things in too much detail.

Variation

The question, "What else about this topic or decision should we consider?" could be listed on a flip chart or poster in the meeting room, and team members could be selected to monitor the discussion each meeting to be sure that a rich discussion is occurring and all viewpoints are heard.

Ask for Commitment

After the meeting, ask, "How might you be willing to use what we discussed today in your daily work?"

EQ 27 Channel Surfing

Level of Risk

Low

Purpose

The purpose of this exercise is to imagine new endings to old situations. By imagining new endings to old or typical situations, we gain the power to change the future. By using the power of our imagination to come up with new endings, we begin the process of mentally rehearsing the situation with a different outcome. Of course, for the outcome to be different, our approach to the situation must also be different. This exercise helps us see that to change the outcome of something, we often need to change our approach.

Why Is This Important?

So often, we get stuck in a rut in our interactions with others. They become predictable because our action and reaction patterns with others are set. Once set, it is difficult to break the expectation and change our behavior. The predictable mindset becomes, if A does or says X, then B will do or say Y. You've heard the expression, "I know what he's going to say, or I know what he will do." The idea of being stuck in predictable patterns means that there is no hope of changing the future, so why bother. Of course, with that attitude, there is no hope of changing the future. So, it leaves us with a choice to look for new endings by changing our behavior toward a situation. By visualizing the new ending, we can work backward to determine how we may behave in a way that may give us a new result.

When to Use This Activity

Use this activity if you find that your team is stuck in a rut or pattern of behavior. Also, use it when you want to help your team develop new norms. This activity will help team members imagine what is possible.

Set the Stage

Ask the team if they have ever been in a situation where they can predict how people will behave. Give an example. Think about simple, common experiences that people repeat on a regular basis. One simple example is the morning routine. Can you predict what others in your family will do each morning? What will they say? What will they do? In what order will they do it? Explain that predictability is fine, but sometimes when it comes to human interaction, breaking predictable patterns could be useful. Ask the team members if they can think of some situations in which breaking the norm or predictable behavior would be desirable. Equate the idea of breaking the norms to changing the channel during a familiar TV rerun and viewing a completely new ending.

Materials

No materials are needed for this activity. Just an active imagination.

The Activity

1. Ask each team member to think about a predictable pattern related to the team's interaction. Guide the team to use real examples, such as what people say when they enter the workplace each morning, who goes to lunch with whom, who is the first to get stressed about the workload, what happens when a mistake is made, and who is the first to crack a joke or smile.

2. Ask each team member to relay a simple scenario about one of the predictable patterns that the team has fallen into. However, this time, ask the team member to change the channel or create a new ending to this familiar scenario.

Key Questions

- What benefit is there to changing the channel on our interactions?
- How can changing the channel create new interactions?
- When we change the channel, do others follow?
- If each of us changed the channel, how could that benefit our team?

- What would happen if you changed the channel on how you react to conflict?
- If you had a particular person that you react to in a negative manner, how could changing the channel change your relationship?

Variation

Use this activity to change the patterns and interactions of the team meeting. You can even experiment with simple things like changing the order of the agenda items to create a new experience. Or ask a different person to facilitate the team meetings. The goal is to change our patterns of interaction to produce a different result. Those different results could surprise you.

Ask for Commitment

After the meeting, ask, "How might you be willing to use what we discussed today in your daily work?"

EQ 28 Voices in Harmony

Level of Risk

Medium

Purpose

The purpose of this exercise is to find team members who experience similar voices as a result of shared experiences and discuss ways in which those voices can be mitigated. However, the focus of this exercise isn't to find partners to share our perspective, but rather to find partners with similar experiences so that together we can build strategies for overcoming voices that can hold us back.

Why Is This Important?

It's important to discuss common flaws and to strategize methods to overcome them; this promotes open communication within the team and an atmosphere of support. It keeps the group focused on self-improvement and encourages people to be open.

When to Use This Activity

This activity can be used after the exercise titled, "Who Said That?" If you have not yet done the exercise "Who Said That?" you'll need to add the steps noted below.

Set the Stage

If you have already done the exercise "Who Said That?" explain that this exercise is the next step in learning more about our voices and ways to mitigate their negative influences by talking with others who share the same voices.

If you haven't done the exercise "Who Said That?" follow the "Set the Stage" instructions for that exercise.

Materials

Index cards and pins.

Worksheet for Eq. 12, "Who Said That." If you haven't done this exercise yet, see Handout 5-3.

The Activity

1. Ask the team members to identify two voices that are very prevalent for them.

2. Ask team members to write each voice on an index card, and pin the index card to their clothing.

3. Ask the group to mingle and find another member who has one of the same voices written on his or her card. (If there are three or four people who share the same voice and would like to work together that's fine.)

4. Once paired, instruct the teammates to answer the following questions:

   a. What does this voice say?
   b. How can this voice interfere with your intentions?
   c. What can you do to mitigate this voice?

5. Now, repeat the above with the second index card.

6. Ask people to take a moment and write the suggestions on how to mitigate this voice on the back of the index card.

   (It is possible that some members will not find someone who has the same voice. If so, they can pair with people who have different voices and answer the same questions.)

Key Questions

- If you were paired with someone who experiences the same voice, how were your voices similar in what they say?
- What was similar about how these voices can get in the way?
- Do you think it is possible to quiet these voices?
- What advice did you gain about what you can do to mitigate these voices?
- Why do you think it is important to quiet these voices?

Variation

After pairing with someone who has the same voice, pair with someone who does not. Share the first two questions:

What does this voice say?
How can this voice interfere with your intentions?

Then, ask the person you are paired with for his or her advice on how to quiet the voice.
Repeat so that each party has an opportunity to discuss.
You can repeat this several times so that each team member gets a variety of advice.

Ask for Commitment

After the meeting, ask, "How might you be willing to use what we discussed today in your daily work?"

EQ 29 Color My World

Level of Risk

Low–Medium

Purpose

The purpose of this exercise is to help team members recall and express various emotions that are present in the workplace. By recalling and expressing these events, participants can learn how to improve their present and future by employing the lessons gained from the past.

Why Is This Important?

Sometimes it's difficult for people to express their thoughts about emotions in the workplace. This exercise is important because it validates the fact that emotions do exist in the workplace, and that emotion makes the events in our lives memorable.

When to Use This Activity

This exercise is very useful if you want a group to acknowledge that emotion plays a significant role in our memories about events. It's also useful to help team members apply lessons from their past to present situations.

Set the Stage

Talk to the group about memory. Explain that we remember facts—including dates, times, and places—about important events. Explain that we also have the ability to recall the emotions associated with important events. (In the United States, most people can recall how they learned the facts about the September 11 attacks, and they can also recall their feelings during that time.) Explain that sometimes, an event is important, not because it was a milestone in our lives, but because of the emotion that we attach to the event—either fondly or not so fondly. Give a personal example of such an experience. Explain that by allowing ourselves the luxury of remembering, we can learn from these experiences and bring our learning to the present.

Materials

Several small slips of colored paper in a fish bowl.
A flip chart listing all of the following color codes:

Proud—Black
Happy—Green
Energized—Brown
Creative—Blue
Angry—Purple
Overwhelmed—Orange
Sad—Yellow
Concerned—Red

The Activity

1. Ask each team member to select a color from the fish bowl.
2. Instruct members to think about a time at work when they experienced the emotion assigned to the corresponding color. Ask members to extract one lesson from the event or memory.
3. Be sure to allow people time to collect their memories about a particular event.
4. Take turns and have members relay their story about the particular event.
5. You can have team members select from the fishbowl more than once.

Key Questions

- Was it difficult to recall a memory or event?
- How can recalling these events help us with our present and future experiences?
- How can we work to create positive emotions in our everyday work?

A Word of Caution

If two team members have had an angry encounter, this activity may bring it to light. If that occurs, you can use this as an opportunity to rebuild the relationship.

Variation

- You can use colored candy.
- You can select one color per meeting and have all team members share a story related to that color.
- You can focus on positive emotions only if the objective is to look for ways to infuse positive emotions into your team.

Ask for Commitment

After the meeting, ask, "How might you be willing to use what we discussed today in your daily work?"

EQ 30 And Now a Word from Our Sponsor

Level of Risk

Low

Purpose

The purpose of this exercise is to raise people's awareness about their strengths and the strengths of their teammates.

Why Is This Important?

It is important for people to recognize their strengths. By recognizing our strengths, we are better able to look for opportunities to use our strengths or to help our team by employing our strengths. Sometimes, because things come easy, we are unaware that they are strengths. This exercise requires us to think about our strengths and verbalize them to others.

When to Use This Activity

Use this exercise to help team members get to know one another. However, it can also be used successfully with an experienced team.

Set the Stage

Tell the group that everyone has strengths and that our combinations of strengths may be unique to us. If you look at yourself as a brand, the unusual combination of your strengths is what differentiates you from others. Marketing professionals are always looking for what differentiates the brand. In other words, what makes one cereal or detergent better or different from the others?

Materials

A piece of poster board for each person.
Magazines.
Markers.
Scissors.

The Activity

1. Instruct participants to create a commercial about themselves that contains two elements: a visual component and a verbal component. For the visual component, team members should select or draw pictures that represent their greatest strengths and why their brand is unusual. For the verbal component, team members should create a 60-second announcement that captures the essence of their strengths and brand.
2. Have each team member share their commercial with the group.

Key Questions

- Was it easy or difficult to come up with a commercial?
- Was anyone uncomfortable talking about your strengths?
- What is the benefit of being aware of our strengths?
- How can you use your strengths in the team?
- How can being aware of others' strengths be useful?
- What can you as a team member do to help people use their strengths?

Variation

- If you have a team who has been together for a long time, you can assign pairs and have each person work on a commercial for the person with whom they are paired. This exercise is very useful for giving people insight about how others see their strengths.
- Instead of pairs, you can do one commercial per meeting and assign the entire team to work on the commercial for each teammate without the input of the person. In this exercise, all members would be asked to think about a teammate's strengths.

Ask for Commitment

After the meeting, ask, “How might you be willing to use what we discussed today in your daily work?”

EQ 31 Emotional Trophies

Level of Risk

Low

Purpose

The purpose of this exercise is to help team members recall positive events or occasions in their lives when they lived up to their intentions or ideals.

Why Is This Important?

Recalling times when we lived up to our intentions reinforces our good intentions. Many small acts throughout the day are purposeful and positive. They create positive interactions and perceptions among our team members.

When to Use This Activity

Use this exercise when the team is feeling defeated, low, or flat. Seek occasions when the team members could use a boost. This exercise is positive and uplifting and affirms so many of the actions that we take for granted in our daily interactions.

Set the Stage

Have you ever heard the expression, "I had good intentions?" Most of us have uttered these words on more than one occasion. Usually, when we say them, it's to announce that we somehow fell short of our goals or intentions. But what about all those times when we don't fall short of our intentions? What about all of those times when we lived up to what we say or promise or intend. Shouldn't those events be noted and celebrated? By celebrating the small things, we can build positive reinforcement, and appreciate ourselves and our teammates. Also, by becoming more aware of the intention to create a positive environment, our actions become more deliberate.

Materials

Trophies—all shapes and sizes. To minimize expense, you can also use pictures of trophies or some other symbol printed on cardstock to represent accomplishments. Because the trophy is just a symbol, anything can do, as long as the group understands the significance of the object.

The Activity

1. Ask team members to recall some task they performed in the last 24 hours that was positive and that they intended to do. (We're looking for simple deeds, like taking out the trash.)
2. After each team member announces his or her event, the other team members should give him or her a paper trophy.
3. Now, ask the team member to recall something in the last 24 hours that they said or did that created a positive interaction with another person. An example would be, "I noticed that Henrietta was busy, so I asked her what I could do to help." As you recall this event, think about your intentions. What were you intending to do? Were you aware of your intention? Did you accomplish your intention?
4. After each team member states his or her example, the other team members should give him or her a paper trophy.
5. Ask each team member to recall something within the last week or month that someone on the team said or did that created a positive interaction.
6. Celebrate by giving the person a trophy.

Key Questions

- Why is it important to note these "emotional trophies?"
- How can these "emotional trophies" reinforce positive interactions in the future?
- What can we do to ensure that our actions live up to our intentions?
- How can being more aware of positive intentions create positive interactions?
- How can you recognize the positive intentions of others?

Variation

Declare every Friday "Positive Intention Day." Ask people to be aware of their positive intentions all day long. By becoming aware of our positive intentions, we are more likely to live them. Awareness of our intentions is the first step toward acting on our intentions.

Ask for Commitment

After the meeting, ask, "How might you be willing to use what we discussed today in your daily work?"

EQ 32 Secret Admirer

Level of Risk

Medium

Purpose

The purpose of this activity is to build positive relationships within the team. It is also very useful for helping people realize their strengths. This exercise also has the benefit of helping people focus on the positive things about others, rather than looking for faults.

Why Is This Important?

When people focus on finding strengths in others, they must shift their viewpoint from critical to grateful. By shifting their viewpoint, they begin to see people in a positive light. Often, people live up to our expectations, so we promote positive actions by seeing people in a positive light. This exercise also gives people the benefit of receiving positive feedback about their behavior from a teammate, which can strengthen the bonds within the team.

When to Use This Activity

Use this activity after the team has worked together for some time. It is also helpful if team members have an opportunity to interact frequently during the course of the day or week.

Set the Stage

All of us have faults, but we also have strengths. If we focus on finding faults in others, it can be easily done. However, it is equally easy to focus on someone's strengths. When we focus on others' strengths, we bring out the best in others. In a team situation, focusing energy on finding strengths in others helps set the stage for positive interactions.

Materials

Index cards (for each team member with the team member's name on it).

A small box or some other object that can be closed, such as bags with a draw string or file boxes) to hold the 3 × 5 index cards.

The Activity

1. Pair participants with a Secret Admirer. (Every participant should be a Secret Admirer and also be observed. If you have an odd number of people in your team, tell the group that someone will be assigned to observe two people.) You have some choices when pairing people:

   a. Have people put their names in a fishbowl and pull a name at random—the name the person picks will be the person that he or she is assigned to observe.
   b. The facilitator assigns people to observe in pairs—in other words, Harry observes Tonita, and Tonita observes Harry.
   c. The facilitator assigns people to observe—Harry observes Tonita, Tonita observes Bonnie, Bonnie observes Jerome, and so on.

2. Do not tell the team member who is assigned to observe him or her. (Hence, the word Secret!)

3. Give each team member twenty index cards.

4. Ask the team members to observe twenty strengths about the person they are assigned to observe and write the strengths on the index card with an example of what they observed. For example, "I observed that Harry is helpful. Harry, without being asked, completed some work from Bonnie when she was called away to a meeting."

5. Instruct the observers to complete the index cards within the next week and place the cards in the box.

6. At team meeting, allow time for the Secret Admirers to review their statements with the person they were assigned to observe.

Key Questions

- ➤ How did you feel when you received the feedback from your Secret Admirer?
- ➤ What did you learn that was a surprise?
- ➤ What did you gain from being a Secret Admirer?
- ➤ What did you gain from being observed?
- ➤ Was it easy or difficult to be a Secret Admirer?
- ➤ How do you think looking for strengths builds a team?
- ➤ How can we make it a habit to look for strengths?
- ➤ Does being observed make us more aware of our behaviors?

A Word of Caution

If you know that two team members do not get along, pairing them can be useful or problematic. Here's what to consider: Do you think the team members would be able to put their differences aside and seriously participate in this exercise? If so, this could be an outstanding exercise to bridge the gap between the pair. If not, it's probably best not to pair them.

Variation

If your team has identified core values, such as treating others with respect, valuing the customers, and so on, you could have the observers look for examples of these values and write down the examples on the index cards to share.

Ask for Commitment

After the meeting, ask, "How might you be willing to use what we discussed today in your daily work?"

EQ 33 Accomplishments Flower Garden

Level of Risk

Low

Purpose

The purpose of this activity is to encourage team members to recognize some of their accomplishments and identify some of their core values and/or characteristics that helped them achieve these successes. As team members become actively engaged in reflecting on their accomplishments, values, and characteristics, they will strengthen their self-awareness.

Why Is This Important?

As people gain self-awareness, their ability to function in a team improves. They gain security by knowing who they are and no longer are challenged by "proving themselves" to others. Also, by improving awareness of the values and characteristics that helped produce success, you can validate these values and characteristics for future use.

When to Use This Activity

Anytime. This exercise can be used as team members are getting to know each other. It can also be used with a team that has been functioning together for some time.

Set the Stage

Tell the group that both on and off the job, we all have accomplishments that we're proud of. Give a personal example. (Try to keep it relatively simple—for example, I painted the bathroom this weekend.) Explain to the group that if you think about your accomplishments, you will discover that success comes from certain values or characteristics that you possess. I painted the bathroom this weekend because of my excellent work ethic, my ability to take risks, and my creativity.

Materials

Paper.
Colored pens/crayons.

The Activity

1. Give each person a piece of paper and a few crayons.
2. Ask teammates to draw a flower garden where the flowers and the roots of the flowers are visible. (If you want, you can do this and copy it. Then have the participants do the labeling and coloring.)
3. Each flower represents an accomplishment. Ask team members to label each flower with an accomplishment. (Coach people to be sure they don't overlook the simple accomplishments that we may take for granted.)
4. Below the surface of the dirt, the roots of the flower represent values or characteristics that enabled the accomplishment to grow. Ask team members to label the roots for each accomplishment.

Key Questions

- Was it difficult or easy to come up with flowers or accomplishments?
- How difficult was it to think about the values or characteristics that you possess, which led to your accomplishments?
- Did you notice any consistent values or characteristics?
- What can we gain from looking at our accomplishments?
- What did you learn about your values or characteristics?
- What values and characteristics are you proud of?
- If you think about things in the future that you would like to accomplish, do you think your values and characteristics can help you?

A Word of Caution

If someone can't think of any accomplishments to list, coach them until they are able to come up with some things they are proud of. Sometimes people just need a little help to think about their successes.

Variation

- You can use this same exercise to focus on team accomplishments. Draw the flowers on flip charts and have the group identify team accomplishments. Then, draw the roots and ask people to think about the team's values or characteristics that led to the accomplishments. This exercise is a great way to visibly celebrate the team's achievements.
- If you think your group may be turned off by the idea of flowers, just change the assignment and have people draw a fishbone. Put the accomplishment at the head of the fish, then write the values or characteristics in the skeleton of the fish.

Ask for Commitment

After the meeting, ask, "How might you be willing to use what we discussed today in your daily work?"

EQ 34 Profiles in Respect

Level of Risk

Medium

Purpose

The purpose of this activity is to help team members verbalize things about their teammates that they respect. By verbalizing these items, the bonds among team members are strengthened.

Why Is This Important?

When teammates respect one another, there is a greater likelihood that people will be sure to come through for one another. Sometimes however, teammates are unaware of how others on the team perceive them.

When to Use This Activity

Use this activity after the team has been together for some time. Team members should have some degree of knowledge about one another.

Set the Stage

Tell the team that they will have an unusual opportunity to give each other feedback. Explain that giving each other positive feedback creates strong bonds within the team.

Materials

Flip chart paper for each team member.
Tape.

The Activity

1. Ask each team member to draw a facial profile or silhouette on a piece of flip chart paper. The profile should be large and should fill the sheet of paper.

2. At the top of the flip chart paper, ask the team members to write their name and the words "Profile of Respect."
3. Hang all of the silhouettes on the walls of the room.
4. Give team members time to circle the room and write what they "like, respect, or prize" about the person on his or her silhouette.
5. Be sure to require that each person write on each person's silhouette. Teammates can choose to sign their contributions or not.
6. Once everyone has had an opportunity to write comments, allow team members time to reflect on their own silhouette.
7. You can also ask team members to stand by their silhouette and read the comments to the team.

Key Questions

- How did you feel when you read the comments on your silhouette?
- Were there any similarities? Any contradictions?
- Was it difficult to write comments for others?
- What is the value of thinking about what we respect, like, or prize about our teammates?

A Word of Caution

Just be sure to require that all team members write on all silhouettes. If not, someone could be embarrassed because they do not have any comments.

Ask for Commitment

After the meeting, ask, "How might you be willing to use what we discussed today in your daily work?"

EQ 35 Perfect Team

Level of Risk

Low

Purpose

The purpose of this exercise is to conceptualize the perfect team. After the team has had an opportunity to think about the perfect team, they can work on actions to move closer to their ideal.

Why Is This Important?

This exercise helps people visualize what the group can become. Once they can see the perfect team, the steps to take to move toward perfection become more apparent. This exercise also gives team members an opportunity to talk about what is important to them as a team member. Sometimes those opinions are not verbalized except loosely around the idea of ground rules. This exercise takes the concept of ground rules and goes much further.

When to Use This Activity

This exercise is useful when a team is first being organizing, but it can also be used at any time to help a team reach its full potential.

Set the Stage

Nothing is perfect. Yet, thinking about the perfect day or the perfect vacation gives us an opportunity to visualize the event in an ideal way. With that ideal in mind, we can take steps to work toward a more perfect outcome. For example, if my ideal is to have a slow and relaxing vacation at the beach, I can't do that in the middle of Kansas. I know I have to take some steps to make that ideal reality. The same is true for our sense of a team and working together. It is very useful to discuss the idea of a perfect team. We may recognize that we have different ideas of what the perfect team is all about, but we may also recognize that we have similarities. These similarities form the common ground that we can work with to make a reality.

Materials

Preselected magazine pictures (If you do some searching, you can find some great images. I try to find images that depict the perfect idea of working together, as well as negative images of work.) If you don't have time for this step, people can conceptualize this in their minds and use words to describe it.

2 flip charts.

The Activity

1. On the top of one flip chart, write "The Perfect Team." On the second flip chart, write "The Perfect Team" with a ∅ symbol drawn through it.
2. Ask team members to individually select pictures that represent their idea of the Perfect Team or pictures that represent the opposite. Each team member should select at least one picture.
3. Ask team members to take turns and explain why they chose the picture they selected.
4. Write words on the flip chart to capture the essence of the team member's idea. Look for action words to describe the Perfect Team's behavior or what the Perfect Team would not do and write these words on the flip chart. Push the group to be specific about the behaviors and give examples. For example, someone might say that the perfect team would support each other. Ask the group members to give an example of how the team would do that.
5. Break the group into groups of three or four and have each small group come up with at least one action the group can agree on that would get them closer to their ideal.
6. Capture the ideas on another piece of flip chart paper.
7. Ask the group members if they could commit to any of the ideas listed on the flip chart paper.
8. Ask group members to state to the group an action they are willing to commit to.

Key Questions

- ➤ Why is it helpful to discuss the Perfect Team?
- ➤ Is everyone's vision of the perfect team the same?
- ➤ What similarities do you see in people's vision of the Perfect Team?
- ➤ What differences do you see in people's vision of the Perfect Team?
- ➤ What can we do about the differences?
- ➤ What can we do to make the vision of the Perfect Team come alive?

A Word of Caution

It is important to give people a sense of both positive and negative behaviors when visualizing the Perfect Team. As the facilitator, if you find that everyone is selecting negative behaviors and the tone of the group seems to be filled with "You shouldn't do this . . . or that . . .," I would suggest asking the team members to restate each negative behavior into a positive behavior. Also, be careful that people don't use this as a way to point fingers at negative behaviors.

Variation

You could extend this to be the Perfect Workplace, the Perfect Company, Perfect Customer Service, or some other ideal related to work.

Ask for Commitment

After the meeting, ask, "How might you be willing to use what we discussed today in your daily work?"

EQ 36 Gut Check

Level of Risk

High

Purpose

The purpose of this exercise is to help the team determine how team members feel about a decision they are about to make. It also forces everyone to take a stand regarding a decision. When a group experiences negative feelings toward a decision, it will impact how well they execute the decision. This exercise will serve the purpose of exposing the concerns that people have.

Why Is This Important?

In business, we try to base our decision on the facts. Therefore, feelings should have nothing to do with the decisions we make. However, it's not that simple. For every decision we make, we generally have some feeling associated with the decision. New research is currently looking at the role feelings play in the decision, but more importantly, how feelings affect the implementation and execution of our decisions. The less enthused people "feel" about the decision, the more likely the execution will be poor or less than satisfactory.

When to Use This Activity

It is recommended that this activity be used with all decisions the group makes. In particular, it should be used when much discussion or debate precedes a decision, thus indicating that several viewpoints exist on the topic.

Set the Stage

Even simple choices or decisions carry feelings associated with them. As you wait for the dinner that you ordered at the local restaurant, you will have feelings that range anywhere from gastro exuberance in anticipation of the arrival of the meal to ambivalence to downright regret. Those feelings can affect how much you enjoy your meal. Decisions at work are no different. It's a good idea to find out how we feel about a decision we are about to make before we make it. By exploring our feelings related to a decision, we could determine if perhaps different alternatives could improve the decision.

Materials

A chart to track decisions and feelings (see Handout 5-11).

The Activity

1. Once the group reaches a decision, ask the group members to put an X on the chart corresponding to how they feel about the decision.
2. Ask group members to indicate whether they agree with the decision or not. (It is certainly possible to agree with a decision even though you may have some negative feelings about it.)
3. Ask the group to analyze the results on the chart.
4. If there is anything negative on the chart, ask if the group could change or modify the decision in any way that would create more positive feelings.

Key Questions

- How are we aligned with our feelings regarding this decision?
- What differences do you see regarding our feelings in this decision?
- If anyone is feeling confusion, what would help them?
- What do you think the data regarding our feelings about this decision might suggest?
- How could the decision be changed or modified to improve the group's acceptance of the decision?
- What can help us to execute this decision despite any negative feelings we may have?

A Word of Caution

Sometimes, the right decision, such as closing a plant or some other decision that will affect personnel, is not necessarily something that the group can feel good about. However, even within the negative context of the decision, people will have some sense as to whether or not they feel the decision is right or wrong. Most of the decisions that your team will be making will probably not fall into the context of these types of decisions. The purpose of this exercise is not to get everyone to feel good about the decision, but rather to explore if/how negative feelings might hamper the execution of the decision and whether or not all feelings have been verbalized. Through this discussion, alternatives may be apparent that are stronger than the decision that currently stands.

Variation

Decisions often evoke mixed emotions. Therefore, you could have members place a 1st and 2nd in the boxes on the chart, to indicate the first and second emotions that they experience related to the decision.

Ask for Commitment

After the meeting, ask, "How might you be willing to use what we discussed today in your daily work?"

HANDOUT 5-11 Tracking Decisions and Feelings

TEAMMATE'S NAME	ANGRY	DISMAYED	ANNOYED	CONCERNED	CONFUSED	NEUTRAL	OK	GOOD	SUPPORTIVE	MOTIVATED	EXCITED	I AGREE WITH THE DECISION.	
												YES	NO
1.													
2.													
3.													
4.													
5.													
6.													
7.													
8.													
9.													
10.													

EQ 37 Timed Reflection

Level of Risk

High

Purpose

The purpose of this activity is to help the team assess its progress. It is very important for team members to have some consistent way to measure how they think the team is functioning. Beyond the tangible measures of the team's accomplishments in terms of quality or cost improvements, this measure gives members an important measure of their interactions.

Why Is This Important?

It's very easy for a team to get stuck in a certain pattern of interaction. When team members consciously focus on and evaluate their interactions, then the team can assess where progress can be made, as well as what should be repeatable and sustainable. Team interactions can't change unless we make an effort to decide on the change. Timed reflection allows us to make that effort.

When to Use This Activity

You can use this activity at several different intervals. You can use it after each meeting, once every other week, or once a month. Less often than once a month is probably not effective.

Set the Stage

Explain to the group that often people interact in the same way for years with no apparent change. If the interaction is working fine, that's great, but if the interaction can be improved and we make no effort to assess the interaction, we may be missing opportunity to improve our interactions. Explain that the purpose of this activity is to help the team assess and evaluate their interactions on a regular basis, with the goal of finding ways to improve.

Materials

The following continuums written on a piece of paper and photocopied so that everyone receives a copy.

Place an X on each continuum to represent your opinion. One represents the lowest score; ten represents the highest.

I feel heard:

____

1 2 3 4 5 6 7 8 9 10

I feel valued:

____

1 2 3 4 5 6 7 8 9 10

My opinions count:

____

1 2 3 4 5 6 7 8 9 10

My contributions are appreciated:

____

1 2 3 4 5 6 7 8 9 10

I feel overworked in relation to everyone else on the team:

____

1 2 3 4 5 6 7 8 9 10

I feel underutilized in relation to everyone else on the team:

____

1 2 3 4 5 6 7 8 9 10

I feel like I belong on the team:

____

1 2 3 4 5 6 7 8 9 10

Name one thing that the team does right.

Name one thing that the team could improve.

The Activity

1. At a prescribed regular time (such as once a month) have each team member quickly complete the survey by placing an X on the continuums and completing the questions. (Instruct the team members to put their X directly on a number so that calculations are simplified.)
2. Calculate the averages on each continuum.
3. Compare and keep a record of the group averages for each continuum.
4. Ask each person to read the item that the team does right and the item that the team could improve.

Key Questions

- How is our group progress?
- What is improving?
- What is stagnant?
- What is declining?
- Ask each person, "What can the team do to make one of your scores increase?"
- What are you willing to commit to doing to improve the scores?

A Word of Caution

If you aren't willing to follow through on this activity, don't do it. It is important that people believe that something will be done with their input. So, be sure to discuss and follow though with suggestions. Your role will be to hold the team accountable for their ideas.

Variation

You could ask people to share their continuum with the team and state why they rated the continuum as they did to gain further insight into the members' concerns.

Ask for Commitment

After the meeting, ask, "How might you be willing to use what we discussed today in your daily work?"

EQ 38 Best Failure

Level of Risk

High

Purpose

The purpose of this exercise is to help people reflect on and learn from their experiences. Just as we learn from Best Practices, we can also learn from each other's failures. By reflecting on and discussing our failures, we also practice being open with our teammates. Best failures also help us frame our failure in a way that is productive by focusing on the lessons learned.

Why Is This Important?

Reflection is critical to greater emotional intelligence. A guided reflection that requires us to frame the experience for the maximum learning potential can be an important tool. Also, sharing our failures with others allows others to learn from our experience and avoid similar mistakes in their lives.

When to Use This Activity

Use this exercise when the group has been together for a while. This exercise has the advantage of bringing purposeful discussion and open communication to a team; therefore, it is useful to use to deepen the team members' relationships.

Set the Stage

Explain to the group that mistakes are one of the best things about life. Mistakes allow us to learn from our experiences. Mistakes also allow us to craft new ways of doing things in the future to avoid repeating errors. However, without the benefit of reflecting on our mistakes, we are often prone to repeating the same mistakes and miss the opportunity to improve. This exercise allows us the luxury of learning from our mistakes and sharing our learning with others. Just as we learn from others' best practices, we can also learn from each other's best failures. Also, tell the group not to be afraid of the word failure. As we learn to embrace the word failure, we become less fearful of failure and more open to learning from mistakes.

Materials

Flip chart or worksheet with prepared questions.

The Activity

1. Instruct team members to think about a failure that they experienced at work. The failure should be something they think went wrong and something they think could have had a different outcome if they had acted in another way.

2. Be sure to remind participants that The purpose of this exercise is to learn from our past, not to cause undue stress or pain from rehashing a failure. In fact, remind participants that our past failures are a gift.

3. Write the following reflection questions on a flip chart or prepare a worksheet with these questions:

   a. Briefly describe the failure.
   b. Why do you consider this a failure?
   c. How do you feel about this failure?
   d. What did you do/not do or say/not say that you think contributed to this failure?
   e. If you could replay this situation, what would you do/say differently?
   f. What did you learn from this failure?
   g. What advice would you give to someone else facing a similar situation?

Key Questions

- ➤ What do we have to gain by focusing on failure?
- ➤ How/why is failure a gift?
- ➤ How can we ensure that we learn lessons from our failures?
- ➤ How can we learn from other people's failures?

A Word of Caution

As the facilitator, be sure to keep the tone and the focus of this lesson on the future. You are using the past to gain skill in our future dealings. Be sure the group knows this and focuses their energy accordingly. Also, instruct the group to choose a failure that they feel comfortable talking about.

Variation

The team can use this exercise to focus on its failures, rather than on individual failures, and what they can learn from these past experiences. Team members should jointly answer the questions. It's interesting to note that team members will differ in their opinions about whether or not an experience was a failure.

Ask for Commitment

After the meeting, ask, "How might you be willing to use what we discussed today in your daily work?"

EQ 39 First Impression

Level of Risk

Medium

Purpose

The purpose of this exercise is to give team members feedback on the first impression they make with others. This exercise allows team members to hear things about the way they come across that they may never have heard before.

Why Is This Important?

Team members should understand that first impressions are important because others often dismiss or judge us based on their first impressions. Although that may be unfair, it's also reality. Therefore, being aware of the first impression that we make can give us important insight. We can decide what we like about our first impressions and if there is anything that we may wish to change.

When to Use This Activity

Use this activity after the group has been together for a short period of time (under 1 year.) Although the exercise can be used with groups that have been functioning for years, it's more difficult for these group members to recall first impressions.

Set the Stage

Explain to the team that there is great value in understanding the first impression that we make on others. Explain that we don't have an opportunity to change our first impression, so giving thought to how we want that first impression to be is critical. By understanding the first impression that we make, we gain valuable insight into the impact we have on others.

Materials

Paper and pencil.

The Activity

1. Have each group member write down his or her thoughts about the first impression he or she makes.
2. Then, select a member to begin. Ask the other team members to think about the first impression they had of this team member.
3. After the team members have given their first impression, ask the teammate to reveal what he or she perceives is his or her first impression.
4. After the first team member has had a turn, take turns until all team members have had an opportunity.
5. Ask team members to complete a worksheet with the following questions:

   a. How accurate was your perception as compared to your teammates'?
   b. What surprised you?
   c. What about your first impression is accurate with who you perceive yourself to be?
   d. What about your first impression is inaccurate with who you perceive yourself to be?
   e. What surprised you?

Key Questions

- How can learning about the first impressions we make be useful?
- Under what circumstances would you want to change your first impression?
- What can we do to change our first impressions?

A Word of Caution

Sometimes we have very negative first impressions of others. It's important that members recognize the spirit of this activity as giving useful feedback. As the facilitator, remind participants to give feedback about qualities or behaviors, not about personal characteristics that people can't change such as size.

Variation

It is useful for teams to discuss first impressions of the organization or the team, as well as individuals. These first impressions of the organization or team are the first ideas that new hires or visitors may see, which may or may not be the way the organization would like to portray itself.

Ask for Commitment

After the meeting, ask, "How might you be willing to use what we discussed today in your daily work?"

EQ 40 I Think; I Feel

Level of Risk

Medium

Purpose

The purpose of this exercise is to help teammates distinguish between thinking and feeling. Both are important in problem solving and decision making, yet people often have trouble recognizing the difference. They also have trouble understanding the roles of both thoughts and feelings in the business arena. This exercise should help clarify those differences and how to use both thoughts and feelings for better results.

Why Is This Important?

It's important to distinguish between thoughts and feelings because both have a place in problem solving and decision making. It's important for a team to recognize the value of both thoughts and feelings and determine how to use both of these independent processes.

When to Use This Activity

You can use this activity any time the group is faced with a decision. The more important the decision, the more useful this activity is.

Set the Stage

Explain that in the business world, some people have been conditioned to leave feelings out of the decision-making and problem-solving processes. This conditioning does not take into account the fact that how we feel about a decision will impact the support we give to a decision, the energy and attention we give it, and how we communicate the decision to others. Also, some people use the words I think when they mean I feel. This exercise helps us to distinguish the two critical functions of thinking and feeling, so that we can use the information in our decision-making process. Explain that thinking comes from the rational brain and involves critical analysis based on facts and data. Explain that feeling comes from the limbic brain and involves our storehouse of information about experiences that we remember and project onto new events or circumstances. Stress the independent nature of thinking and feeling. Give a personal example to separate the two.

Materials

Flip chart and markers.

The Activity

1. When the group is faced with a decision, ask each member to state his or her thoughts as well as feelings about the available options.
2. Capture each member's thoughts and feelings in separate columns on a flip chart.

I think . . .	I feel . . .
Example: I think 4% of customers will reject the higher price based on the analysis we did on price last January.	Example: I fear that if people reject the higher price, we could be faced with a decline in sales.

Key Questions

- How can examining both thoughts and feelings help us make better decisions?
- How can uncovering feelings improve the execution of our decisions?

Variation

You can have group members write their answers on index cards and then pass them forward for discussion. Also, if the group is considering more than one option regarding a particular decision, the group can be asked to write their responses to the options.

Ask for Commitment

After the meeting, ask, "How might you be willing to use what we discussed today in your daily work?"

EQ 41 Cartoon Characters

Level of Risk

Low

Purpose

The purpose of this exercise is to improve self-awareness. It is also useful to help team members understand each other. Finally, cartoon characters can help us smile and think about ourselves with humor.

Why Is This Important?

Developing a sense of humor about yourself and your life's situations can help redirect your emotional response. Humor stops us from taking ourselves too seriously. It's a useful way to reduce stress and enjoy the ride. Also, in a team where members are playful and develop a sense of humor, creativity and innovation are more likely to flourish.

When to Use This Activity

This activity is useful for teams whose members do not know one another very well. It is also useful for teams who have been working together for a while.

Set the Stage

Explain to the group that when we can see ourselves and the world through humor, we are less likely to have negative emotional reactions. It's difficult to laugh and be angry or fearful at the same time. Therefore, humor is a very powerful way to help us gain perspective. Explain that cartoon characters are funny because they exaggerate qualities or traits that people share. Tell the group that by looking for ourselves in cartoon characters, we can gain powerful insight and self-awareness. We will also have the joy of laughing at some of our characteristics. The facilitator should be prepared to give personal examples of cartoon characters with whom he or she identifies.

Materials

Comics section of the newspaper, pictures of cartoon characters—the more variety the better.

The Activity

1. Ask the team members to think about a cartoon character that has a trait or characteristic that they identify with.

2. Instruct the team to think about the personality of the characters, not the physical characteristics of the characters. (Dumbo, because he has big ears, is not what we're looking for.) Instead, we're looking for the characteristics or traits of Dumbo. An example would be Dumbo, because he didn't have the confidence to believe that he could fly.

3. Taking turns, ask each team member to talk about the cartoon character he or she selected and to explain why.

4. After each team member reveals the cartoon character he or she selected, ask the rest of the team if they agree with the selection. Ask them to state why or why not. You'll have to decide if you think the team is ready for the feedback from this type of interaction.

Key Questions

- How can looking at ourselves through the eyes of humor help us?
- Why is humor effective at mitigating negative reactions such as anger or fear?
- When is humor helpful and when is it harmful? (Humor directed at ourselves is fine. Laughing at others is not appropriate.)
- How can we use humor in our team to help one another?
- How can humor disrespect others?
- What happens to our mood when we laugh at ourselves?

A Word of Caution

Be sure the team gets the message that humor directed at oneself is okay, but that humor directed at others is not. The intention of this exercise is to help us lighten up when looking at ourselves and not take ourselves too seriously. It is not to poke fun at others.

Variation

- A variation of this exercise would be to use characters from movies or books.
- Another possibility is to have team members assign characters to each other. The big caution here is to be sure the team does this in a constructive manner and not in a mean spirited way. You'd have to be careful with this one. For example, if someone assigns Cruella DeVille to a teammate, it's more than likely uncomplimentary and destructive. You could also have team members bring in pictures of the characters they relate to and hang them at their workstations as a reminder to lighten up.
- Another fun variation of this exercise is to ask the team members to think about a cartoon character that they would like to identify with and ask them to explain why. For example, "I would like to identify with Garfield because he represents a nonchalant attitude about things that I would like to have instead of taking things too seriously and intensely."

Ask for Commitment

After the meeting, ask, "How might you be willing to use what we discussed today in your daily work?"

EQ 42 Throwing Rocks

Level of Risk

Medium

Purpose

The purpose of this exercise is to help the team think about traits or interactions that may hold it back from accomplishing its mission. This exercise allows team members to identify and visually discard things that hold them back.

Why Is This Important?

It is important for team members to identify the traits or interactions that are holding them back. It is even more important for the participants to consciously decide that they would be better off if they discarded these things. By connecting this to a physical item, it reinforces the idea that the team has decided to discard the trait or interaction.

When to Use This Activity

Use this exercise when you think the team has some obvious weaknesses in terms of a trait or interaction that it should let go. This exercise is also useful as a follow-up exercise to "Five Key Weaknesses."

Set the Stage

Ask the team members to think about their interactions as a team. Ask them to identify qualities or characteristics that they think are holding them back. (If you've done the exercise Five Key Weaknesses, you can draw on the data from that exercise.) Explain that sometimes our team weaknesses need to be overcome by acquiring new skills, but sometimes weaknesses are traits or interactions that as a team we just must decide are not in our best interests and decide to throw them away. For example, if our team lacks analytical skills, we may need to gain some expertise and training. However, if one of our team weaknesses is that we criticize team members' ideas instead of fully listening, it would benefit the team to stop this destructive behavior.

Materials

River rocks and magic markers.

The Activity

1. Ask the team to think about traits or interactions that are holding it back from reaching its full potential. (If you've already done the exercise Five Key Weaknesses, let the team review these weaknesses.)
2. Ask the team to agree on traits or interactions that it would like to throw away.
3. Each team member should take a rock for each item they have chosen to throw away and write it on the rock using a magic marker.
4. Take the team to an outdoor location, preferably by a body of water and have them hurl the rocks into the water as symbolism that the team has decided to throw away this item. The team could do each item in unison. For example the leader could say, "Let's throw our tendency to criticize away."

Key Questions

- How can deciding to throw away certain characteristics improve our performance?
- Why is letting go of something important sometimes?
- What can we learn from letting go of certain things?
- How can team members help one another to let go of certain things?

A Word of Caution

People and windows! Just to reiterate what we learned in kindergarten, don't throw stones at or near people. It's best to do this exercise outside and away from any windows too. The last thing we want is to harm people or destroy the place.

DO NOT LET THE TEAM WRITE DOWN NAMES ON THE ROCKS. This exercise is not about letting go of people that the team feels are holding them back from reaching its goals. That's the purpose of performance management.

Variation

Team members can select traits or characteristics in their own behavior that they would like to eliminate. Just have team members think about themselves and write down something that is interfering with their ability to be their best. Instruct them to write it on the stone, tell the group why they would like to let go of it and hurl it into the water.

Ask for Commitment

After the meeting, ask, "How might you be willing to use what we discussed today in your daily work?" Also, asking, "Didn't we throw that away?" provides a powerful reminder that can be used in future team meetings to remind team members of items they decided to let go of.

EQ 43 The Pause Button

Level of Risk

Low

Purpose

The purpose of this exercise is to help people stop undesirable behavior before it occurs. By helping people recognize "in the moment" when they are experiencing an undesirable emotional reaction, this exercise gives people a visual aid to slow down their reaction time.

Why Is This Important?

It is important for people to know when they are at risk for undesirable behavior. When that risk occurs, it's important for people to have a mechanism to help slow down their reaction time so they can think about an appropriate response. Too often, we react to events rather than think about the reaction that is most aligned with our intentions or values. When we have an opportunity to think about the values or reaction that would be most useful in a particular situation, we are more apt to behave in a way that is consistent with these values or intentions. The idea here is to reduce the amount of time when we are reacting to situations and replace that with thoughtful action.

When to Use This Activity

Use this activity when the team is experiencing conflict. You can also use this activity following the PFAT scan exercises, so that team members recognize that they have a choice and a tool to use to shape their actions and words. This exercise is very effective during an actual conflict.

Set the Stage

Ask team members if they have ever experienced a time when they regretted something they said or did. (Most of us can readily think about times when this occurred.) Now, ask the team members if they knew at the time, that the situation was not going very well. (Often people will say in retrospect, "I knew when I was saying so and so, that it was the wrong thing to say, but I just couldn't help it." Or, I don't know what came over me.") Give a personal example. Explain that the reason we sometimes feel powerless over our words or actions is because we don't stop and give ourselves power. Power comes from thoughtful action. When we allow ourselves the luxury of thoughtful action, we gain mastery over our reactions and emotions. Also, explain to the group that thoughtful action takes very little time compared with the time it takes to undo the effects of undesirable action.

Materials

A visual representation of a PAUSE button. The visual representation could be a large PAUSE button drawn on a flip chart, or an actual button, that people could press sitting in the center of the meeting table. (I use a large piece of foam covered with red cloth and white letters that say PAUSE.)

The Pause Predictor Worksheet (see Handout 5-12).

The Activity

1. Explain to the group the concept of a 10-second pause as a technique to slow down our reaction time. Introduce the PAUSE button.
2. Explain that during the PAUSE stage, our intentions should be to place the interaction on PAUSE and to visualize a different outcome—an outcome that would be aligned with our values and intentions.
3. Divide the team into pairs by asking people to align on opposite sides of an issue.
4. You can use the list of topics that you prepared for the PFAT Scan exercise. (Better yet, use an actual work related topic where people have strong differences of opinion. The difficulty will increase when you use actual work topics.)
5. Ask the pairs to begin discussion. Instruct the pairs to discuss the issue and when someone feels they are at risk for a negative response, ask them to press the pause button.

6. Instruct members to complete the worksheet when the pause button is pressed.

Key Questions

- When we think about our intention, does it sometimes lead us to change our response choice?
- What is our intention in a conflict situation? (Is it to win? Is it to be heard? Is it to demoralize our opponent? Is it to disrespect our opponent?)
- How can changing a response choice change the outcome of an interaction?
- What signals did you encounter that caused you to press the pause button?
- Is the purpose of PAUSE to avoid a conflict? (No, it is to help members understand that conflict is healthy and can lead to differences of opinion that lead to improved problem solving. The purpose of pausing is to ensure that the way we interact during a conflict allows continued discussion rather than shutting off communication and respect.)
- What's the difference between avoiding conflict and redirecting your response?

Variation

To practice this concept, you can ask participants to complete the worksheet based on a past conflict. The participants could think about a past conflict that didn't have a positive outcome. They could reflect on what they said and then brainstorm other possible responses. (Brainstorming could be done with another person or in a small group.)

Ask for Commitment

After the meeting, ask, "How might you be willing to use what we discussed today in your daily work?" This is a very powerful concept to use during team meetings. By using a visual such as a PAUSE button during team meetings, the team is reminded to step back and consider their intentions, responses, and outcomes.

HANDOUT 5-12 The Pause Predictor Worksheet

My intention:	
Response Choice 1	Possible Outcome 1
Response Choice 2	Possible Outcome 2
Response Choice 3	Possible Outcome 3
Response Choice 4	Possible Outcome 4
Response Choice 5	Possible Outcome 5
Which response will produce the outcome that most closely matches your intention?	

EQ 44 The Pause Elf

Level of Risk

Medium

Purpose

The purpose of this exercise is to help team members recognize the signs that indicate the need for a pause. Sometimes it is difficult to recognize when these signs are brewing in ourselves; however, others are often aware of these signs before we are. Therefore, by assigning someone to watch for these signs and having that person press the PAUSE button for us, we begin to learn to recognize signs in ourselves that require a PAUSE. The other benefit of this exercise is that we become more aware of our own behavior when we are assigned to observe it in others.

Why Is This Important?

As we become adept at self-management, it is important for us to be able to recognize signs that signal when a PAUSE is required. This exercise helps us to recognize "in the moment" when a PAUSE is necessary.

When to Use This Activity

Use this activity when teammates are likely to engage in undesirable behavior and people are likely to say things that do not produce positive outcomes. Use this technique to help the team members develop their own self-management skills.

Set the Stage

Explain that sometimes others are aware that a situation or conflict is brewing before the person engaging in the conflict is aware of it. Explain that the purpose of this exercise is to help our teammates by observing signs that they are at risk for a hijacking and therefore require a PAUSE. By helping others know when they are at risk for a hijacking, we are better able to understand our own signals that put us at risk for undesirable behavior.

Materials

A visual representation of a PAUSE button. The visual representation could be a large PAUSE button drawn on a flip chart, or an actual button, that people could press sitting in the center of the meet ing table. (I use a large piece of foam covered with red cloth and white letters that say PAUSE.)

The Activity

1. Ask each person to select a PAUSE Elf. The PAUSE Elf should be someone that the teammate thinks has good observation skills and whose opinion the teammate will accept.
2. Instruct the Pause Elf to press the PAUSE button any time during a team meeting, when he or she believes the person he or she is assigned to observe is at risk for a hijacking.

Key Questions

- Was the team member aware of the need to PAUSE before the Pause Elf pointed it out?
- What signals did the Pause Elf read that indicated a need for PAUSE?
- What signals were present in the team member being observed?
- What alternative behavior would have been useful for the team member to employ?

A Word of Caution

You don't want to use this exercise for a long period of time. Just use it long enough to help team members gain awareness of their need for a PAUSE. If you use it too long, you may be creating a dependency on others rather than self-management and self-observation. However, initially it is very useful to help team members know when they require a PAUSE.

Variation

A variation of this exercise would be to appoint one person per team meeting to be the Pause Elf and to press the PAUSE button, when he or she observes any team member who may be at risk for a hijacking. The benefit to this variation is that it allows each team member to observe the entire team. It also allows each team member to concentrate on building his or her observation skills.

Ask for Commitment

After the meeting, ask, "How might you be willing to use what we discussed today in your daily work?"

EQ 45 Best Practices

Level of Risk

Low

Purpose

The purpose of this exercise is to help the team recognize and celebrate its best practices. The team can use the Best Practices exercise to highlight their accomplishments and to learn about the elements that were present, which contributed to the best practice.

Why Is This Important?

By focusing and reflecting on Best Practices, the team can reinforce positive team behaviors that led to the accomplishment. In addition, celebration serves the purpose of recognizing the team's hard work.

When to Use This Activity

Use this exercise when the group has been together for a while. This exercise can be used when the team has had a dry spell regarding accomplishments. It can also be used when the team is facing a particularly challenging assignment because it can serve the purpose of helping the team identify its strong points.

Set the Stage

Explain to the team that periodically it's important to step back and recognize the accomplishments of the team. By stepping back and recognizing accomplishments, the team can reinforce positive behaviors so that team members can repeat the behaviors in the future. Celebrating accomplishments is also fun.

Materials

Flip chart or worksheet with prepared questions.

The Activity

1. Instruct team members to brainstorm about their best practices. The best practices should be something they think they successfully executed, and they should have performance evidence that suggests a best practice. The team should select three items that they think best exemplify "Best Practices."

2. Remind participants to look at the team's accomplishments, not the accomplishments of individuals.

3. For each best practice that the team selects, ask participants to address the following questions on a flip chart or prepare a worksheet with these questions:

   Briefly describe the best practice.
   Why do you consider this a best practice?
   How do you feel about this best practice?
   What did the team do that contributed to this best practice?
   What can we learn from this best practice?
   What can we bring from this best practice to the problem/issue that we are currently facing?

4. Finally, ask the team members to find a way to celebrate or commemorate their Best Practices. (Some teams put up a bulletin board complete with lessons learned, others give trophies, and others celebrate with cake and ice cream.)

Key Questions

- What do we have to gain by focusing on our best practice?
- How can we ensure that we continue the qualities that contributed to our best practice?

Variation

The team can do a comparison of some of its best practices and its best failures. The members can analyze what elements were present in the best practices and what elements were present in the best failures and learn what to reinforce and what to avoid. The team jointly should answer the questions listed above. It's interesting to note that team members will differ in their opinions about whether or not an experience was a failure or success.

Ask for Commitment

After the meeting, ask, "How might you be willing to use what we discussed today in your daily work?"

Heroes

Level of Risk

Low

Purpose

The purpose of this exercise is to celebrate qualities in ourselves that are similar to qualities in people we admire.

Why Is This Important?

It's important to recognize our positive characteristics, not in a boastful way, but in a reinforcing way. If there are positive things we admire in others, then recognizing these qualities in ourselves will reinforce these qualities.

When to Use This Activity

You can use this activity at any time during the team meetings. It's appropriate for getting to know one another and also can be used with team members who know each other well.

Set the Stage

We all have people whom we admire. Our heroes can be famous or ordinary people, living or dead, fictional or nonfictional. Each of these heroes has characteristics or qualities that we admire. Sometimes we admire things in our heroes that we do not see in ourselves; other times, we admire things in our heroes that we occasionally see in ourselves. Our heroes remind us of our ideal self—of the self that we would like to see more of if things didn't get in the way.

Materials

Hero buttons or hero tags.

The Activity

1. Instruct the group members to think about someone they consider a hero.
2. Ask the group members to list the qualities they admire about their hero.
3. Next, ask group members to think about a time when they exhibited some of these same qualities.
4. Ask group members to share their examples with the group.
5. After each person has given their example, give them a hero button.

Key Questions

- How did it feel to recognize that you and your hero had something in common?
- What can you learn from your hero?
- Why is it important to celebrate the qualities in ourselves that we admire in our heroes?
- What holds you back from displaying these qualities more often?
- What can you do to overcome the obstacles that hold you back from displaying these qualities more often?

A Word of Caution

Some people may be uncomfortable because they may consider this boasting. Help them distinguish between boasting and identifying and celebrating positive qualities.

Variation

If the group is large, the examples and the questions can be done in pairs or triads.

Ask for Commitment

After the meeting, ask, "How might you be willing to use what we discussed today in your daily work?"

EQ 47 It's in the Air

Level of Risk

Low

Purpose

A powerful technique for managing negative emotions and allowing time to consider our reactions to such emotions is breathing. Deep breathing has long been touted as a way to relax and with good reason. The purpose of this exercise is to practice the breathing technique that can be used by any team member to step back and gain perspective, so that he or she can think about a situation rather than react emotionally and, perhaps, regretfully.

Why Is This Important?

Proper breathing slows our limbic reactions and allows the rational portion of our brain time to catch up and consider the proper and most productive response to an emotional situation.

When to Use This Activity

This activity is useful at any time with the team. It is particularly useful when the team is overworked or stressed. It's also very useful if team members tend to have short triggers and need a tool to help them scale back their emotional reactions to each other.

Set the Stage

We've all been breathing since birth, yet we may be able to improve and gain tremendous benefits from practicing a form of breathing that is known to relax and slow our emotional responses. Deep breathing has been proven to have health benefits and reduce stress. Deep breathing can be practiced anywhere and by anyone. Explain that deep breathing is an excellent tool to use when you are feeling stress, anger, fear, or overwhelmed at work.

Materials

No materials are needed for this activity.

The Activity

Instruct the group on the technique of deep breathing. The technique includes:

1. Sit in a comfortable position.
2. Close your mouth.
3. Draw in a long, slow, deep breath through your nose while counting to eight.
4. Take your breath all the way down to your belly. (You can put your hand on your stomach to feel it expand.)
5. Exhale through your mouth slowly and gently.
6. Repeat several times.

Key Questions

- ➤ How do you feel after practicing this breathing technique?
- ➤ When do you think this technique can be useful?
- ➤ What can we do to remind ourselves to breathe deeply?
- ➤ How can breathing deeply improve our team's interactions?

Variation

You can open or close team meetings with this breathing exercise. You can also use it as a break during a team meeting. If you find your team in a particularly heated discussion, you can stop the discussion and take a breather break. (The expression, "Take a breather," can have a literal meaning here.)

Ask for Commitment

After the meeting, ask, "How might you be willing to use what we discussed today in your daily work?"

EQ 48 My Mantra

Level of Risk

Low

Purpose

The purpose of this exercise is to encourage each team member to adopt a phrase or statement that he or she finds useful to help him or her gain mastery and self-control over negative emotions or situations where they feel anger, fear, or another emotion that could create a negative situation if that emotion were acted upon without thought.

Why Is This Important?

It's important that each team member finds words that he or she can use to improve his or her mastery over emotional reactions. As people gain mastery over their emotional reactions, they are no longer victims of their emotions. Instead, they now have control over how they choose to express themselves. A mantra is a critical phrase that can be used to shift a person's emphasis from the limbic to rational thought.

When to Use This Activity

You can use this activity at any time. It is particularly useful when the group seems to be experiencing and expressing negative emotions in a manner that is destructive to teamwork. This exercise is also very productive to follow the exercise on breathing (It's in the Air) because these two techniques work together to produce a different emotional response.

Set the Stage

Ask the group members if they have ever experienced an emotional reaction, such as anger and later had the thought, "Gee, it seemed more important at the time, than it does now." Or perhaps you found that you can't even remember the specific incident that raised your ire, you just remember the ire. Chances are, if that's the case, you probably overreacted. Just imagine if you had a magic wand that you could wave that would calm your reaction so that you have a chance to gain perspective and select a reaction that is more appropriate to your intentions. Well, you do. That magic wand is the use of a mantra. A mantra is nothing more than a phrase, sentence, or question that you say to yourself to calm your limbic reaction and allow your rational thought to kick in.

Materials

Index cards and magic markers.

The Activity

1. Give the definition of a mantra and some examples of mantras:

   Ex: Is this the hill I want to die on?
   In the scheme of life is this really important?
   Am I even going to remember this five years from now?
   Let it go!
   He/she isn't aiming at me, I'm just getting fallout.

2. Ask each team member to devise his or her own mantra. The mantra should be something that makes sense and helps the team member gain perspective and stay calm.

3. Team members can write their mantras on the index cards provided, and place the cards in front of them so they can see their mantra during team meetings.

Key Questions

- How can a mantra help you?
- How can it help our team?
- Why does using a mantra give us a different perspective?
- How can using a mantra with deep breathing help our team interaction?

A Word of Caution

Mantras should not be a negative statement about other people. For example, a statement that could give you calm and change your perspective could be, "Everyone is an idiot." However, that would not set us up for redirecting our emotions in a positive way. The mantra should help us to redirect our future actions in a positive manner.

Variation

Some teams have decided to write a team mantra. One team that I worked with decided to use the mantra, "Let's help, and not hurt one another." They pasted it on the wall of their team meeting room and pointed to it any time things seemed to heat up.

Ask for Commitment

After the meeting, ask, "How might you be willing to use what we discussed today in your daily work?"

EQ 49 Flying Values

Level of Risk

High

Purpose

The purpose of this activity is to help the team recognize when their values are at risk of being compromised. Most teams/companies have stated values. These values are generally well stated and may contain words and statements such as, Respectful of all Coworkers; Honesty and Integrity in All Our Interactions; Superior Customer Service; and so on. This activity will serve to reinforce the values and to point out occasions when our values are not being implemented. (You must have stated values to do this activity. If you do not have stated values, consider creating some as a team.)

Why Is This Important?

Values serve as our guides. They help us to determine how we should behave in the company or on our team. However, values often get compromised. Superior Customer Service deteriorates when the customer asks for something outside of the ordinary. Respect for coworkers may disappear when the coworker is disrespectful toward you. These breaches in our values erode our interactions.

When to Use This Activity

This activity is very useful after the team has been functioning for some time. You'll need to have some history to come up with examples of when the values are at risk.

Set the Stage

Discuss the importance of having stated values to guide the team's interactions. Values serve the purpose of creating a blueprint for interactions. If we say that we value a respectful workplace, then we must work to determine how we must behave to live by that value. However, if I'm unaware of what you perceive to be respectful, then I could unintentionally be disrespectful toward you. Therefore, discussing values and how the team can live up to its values is important. It's also important to understand when and under what circumstances the team is not living up to its values.

Materials

Paper airplanes with the company or team's values written on the wings.

The Activity

1. Have each team member think about an example of when the team did not fully live its values.
2. Each team member should select an airplane with the value written on it that relates to his or her example.
3. The team member should relay the example to the team. After he or she relays the example, he or she should fly the paper airplane to symbolize the values crash.

Key Questions

- What is the impact of too many crashes on our team's values?
- What's the benefit of discussing examples of when our team didn't live its values?
- How can we learn from our values mistakes?
- What can we do to prevent values crashes?

A Word of Caution

This activity is powerful. If your team is honest, some important conflicts can surface. Be sure to give team members time to discuss the examples. Focus the discussion on what the team can learn from their responses. Most of the time, people are well intentioned, but they are unaware of how others may perceive a certain action. This exercise can serve as an eye opener.

Variation

You can make this activity a planning activity for a new team. Ask the team to identify the values that they would like to adopt. Then, ask each team member to state an example of what it would be like if people were not living the value. What behaviors would people engage in that would sabotage the values and cause a crash?

Ask for Commitment

After the meeting, ask, "How might you be willing to use what we discussed today in your daily work?"

EQ 50 What's Different?

Level of Risk

Medium

Purpose

The purpose of this exercise is to help participants reflect on how they have changed. By getting people to recognize how they have changed over a period of time, participants are able to understand that they can continue to change. It's useful however, for participants to realize that change doesn't have to be accidental; it can be a planned event.

Why Is This Important?

Sometimes people believe that change is not possible. However, most people will quickly recognize that they are somehow different than they were years ago.

When to Use This Activity

This activity is useful when a team is getting to know one another; however, it is also useful for teams that have been together for some time. This activity is particularly useful if you are trying to form deeper relationships among team members to create a better understanding of one another.

Set the Stage

Bring in a children's puzzle that shows two similar pictures that, upon close examination, have minor differences. Show the team an old picture of you and a current picture of you. Explain that many things are the same about the pictures; after all, you're the same person. However, explain that many things are also different. (You can lightheartedly refer to graying temples, bifocals, different hairstyles, and so on.) However, rather than the visible differences, talk about the invisible differences in the picture. Talk to the group about how you are different than you were when the earlier photo was taken.

Materials

Ask participants to bring in an old photo. You can ask everyone to bring in his or her senior picture from high school. Or, you could designate a year and ask everyone to bring in an old photo from that year. Obviously, you'll need to take into consideration the age of your group.

The Activity

1. Ask people to make a list of how they are different from the person who appears in the photo. Ask the people to list how they have changed since the earlier photo was taken. Ask people to determine if they think they have changed for the better or not.
2. Ask each team member to share his or her picture and talk about how he or she has changed.

Key Questions

- How many of you planned the changes you discussed?
- Do you think you will continue to change in the next 10 years? 20 years?
- How can thinking about the person we wish to become be useful to our growth?
- How can we facilitate a planned change in the person we wish to become?

Variation

You can ask people to speak to others who have known them for a long time and get feedback on how they have changed over the years.

Ask for Commitment

After the meeting, ask, "How might you be willing to use what we discussed today in your daily work?"

Recommended Resources

Blanchard, Ken and Michael O'Connor. *Managing By Values.* San Francisco, Berrett-Koehler Publishers, 1997.

Canfield, Jack and Jacqueline Miller. *Heart at Work Stories and Strategies for Building Self-Esteem and Reawakening the Soul at Work.* New York: McGraw-Hill, 1996.

Chermiss, Cary and Adler, Mitchel. *Promoting Emotional Intelligence in Organizations.* American Society for Training and Development, 2000.

Conger, Jay A. *The Charismatic Leader.* San Francisco: Jossey-Bass Publishers, 1992.

Cooper, Robert K. and Ayman Sawaf. *Executive EQ Emotional Intelligence in Leadership and Organizations.* New York: The Berkley Publishing Group, 1997.

Covey, Stephen. *Principle-Centered Leadership.* New York: Summit Books, 1990.

Goleman, Daniel. *Emotional Intelligence Why it can matter more than IQ.* New York: Bantam Books, 1995.

———. *Working With Emotional Intelligence.* New York: Bantam Doubleday Dell Pub.

Goleman, Daniel, Boyatzis, Richard and McKee, Annie. *Primal Leadership.* Cambridge, MA: Harvard Business School Press, 2002.

Harmon, Frederick G. *Playing for Keeps.* New York: John Wiley & Sons Inc., 1996.

Hawley, Jack. *Reawakening the Spirit in Work.* New York: Simon & Schuster, 1993.

Herman, Stanley M. *The Tao at Work.* San Francisco: Jossey-Bass Publishers, 1994.

Jones, Laurie Beth. *Jesus CEO.* New York: Hyperion, 1995.

Kaye, Les. *Zen at Work.* New York: Crown Trade Paperbacks, 1996.

Kelley, Robert E. *How to be a Star at Work.* New York: Times Business, Random House, 1998.

Kouzes, James and Barry Posner. *The Leadership Challenge.* San Francisco: Jossey-Bass Publishers, 1987.

Lynn, Adele B. *In Search of Honor—Lessons From Workers on How to Build Trust.* BajonHouse Publishing, 1998.

———. *The EQ Difference: A Powerful Plan for Putting Emotional Intelligence to Work.* New York: AMACOM, 2005.

———. *The Emotional Intelligence Activity Book.* New York: AMACOM, 2001.

Salovey, Peter, PhD, and John Mayer, PhD. *Emotional Development and Emotional Intelligence.* New York: Basic Books, 1997.

Sashkin, Marshall. *Becoming a Visionary Leader.* King of Prussia, PA: Organization Design and Development, 1986.

Sterrett, Emily. *The Managers Pocket Guide to Emotional Intelligence.* HRD Press, 2000.

Wall, Bob. *Coaching for Emotional Intelligence: The Secret to Developing the Star Potential in Your Employees.* New York: AMACOM, 2006.

Weisinger, Hendrie, PhD. *Emotional Intelligence at Work.* San Francisco: Jossey-Bass, 1997.

Index

About the Author

Adele B. Lynn is the founder of The Adele Lynn Leadership Group, an international consulting and training firm that helps leaders forge trusting relationships. She is a frequent keynote speaker who inspires leaders to create and manage the emotional climate of their organizations for greater results. Her company also provides resource methods for trainers and coaches to guide organizations toward greater emotional intelligence and high trust. Her previous books on emotional intelligence include *The Emotional Intelligence Activity Book* and *The EQ Difference.* She lives in Belle Vernon, Pennsylvania.

For more information contact:

The Adele Lynn Leadership Group
609 Broad Ave.
Belle Vernon, PA 15012
724 929-5352
www.lynnleadership.com